THE KISTE AND OG

SERIES IN ANT

Editors

ROBERT C. KISTE   EUGENE OGAN

University of Minnesota

Robert C. Kiste was born and raised in Indiana. After
completing his undergraduate studies in anthropology at
Indiana University in 1961, he took his graduate training
at the University of Oregon, where his Ph.D. in anthropology was awarded in 1967. In the same year, he moved to
the University of Minnesota where he now has an appoint-
ment as associate professor of anthropology. While on
sabbatical leave during the 1972-73 academic year, he
taught at the University of Hawaii. Dr. Kiste's specializa-
tions and interests include social and cultural change, the
history of anthropology, and Oceania, particularly Micronesia. Among his current professional memberships are
the American Anthropological Association, the Association
for Social Anthropology in Oceania, and the Society for
Applied Anthropology.

THE BIKINIANS

 Cummings Publishing Company

A Study in Forced Migration

ROBERT C. KISTE

University of Minnesota

Menlo Park, California · Reading, Massachusetts
London · Amsterdam · Don Mills, Ontario · Sydney

Cover Photo. Atomic cloud during Baker Day Blast (July 25, 1946) at Bikini. This fifth atomic bomb at Bikini was recorded by an automatic camera from a nearby island.

Cummings Publishing Company, Inc.
2727 Sand Hill Road
Menlo Park, California   94025

For Len and those three—
Val, Vince, and Hazel—
who were patient while
he and I were concerned
with Bikinians

Foreword

Common to all of the monographs in this series is a concern with social and cultural change. Each is a description based on original field research which contains features creating a distinct intellectual and emotional impact. Robert Kiste's book about the men, women, and children who were moved from Bikini atoll in the Pacific is significant, I believe, in at least two ways.

First, Kiste makes a contribution to the anthropology of colonialism. University students who make up a major part of the series' audience may not be accustomed to thinking of the United States as a colonial power, and certainly, the American presence in the Marshall Islands has little to do with the kinds of exploitation, for example, of cheap labor or raw materials, which characterized imperialism before World War II. However, as a number of social scientists have begun to point out, there is more than one variety of colonialism. The Bikinians provide an example of an essentially defenseless people who have been callously shoved from one island to another in order to meet the political and military goals of aliens to whom a tiny but originally vital community is simply irrelevant.

Second, Kiste's meticulously detailed data about land, power, privilege, and influence provide splendid examples of what anthropologists call "extended case studies" in political anthropology. The student who reads Chapters Three through Seven carefully will receive insights into important anthropological problems which are not so easily accessible in studies that emphasize a generalized "homeostatic-functionalist" treatment of the complexities and conflicts of ongoing social life.

There are issues in the Bikini case which will not disappear with a wave of the not-so-magic wand of Western technology. Kiste and the anthropologists whose work he cites have laid bare the human dilemma produced when a colonial or neo-colonial power disrupts a traditional culture. Platitudes about "applied anthropology" shrivel beneath the heat of human misery.

Kiste has been painfully honest in his description of a quarter-century's bungling with Bikinians' lives. Is it possible to draw lessons from this case and to avoid such guilt and distress in future contacts between "superpowers" and more traditional societies? I suggest that readers of this book will ponder that question for some time to come.

University of Minnesota　　　　　　　　　　　EUGENE OGAN
Minneapolis, Minnesota　　　　　　　　　　*Series Co-Editor*
July, 1974

Acknowledgments

In the process of developing this study, I have been indebted to many people. Michael Hamnett (University of Hawaii), Michael Lieber (University of Illinois-Chicago Circle), William T. Stuart (University of Maryland), Alan Rew (University of Minnesota), and Michael Rynkiewich (Macalester College) have read portions of the manuscript at different stages of its writing. Their criticisms have always been constructive, and as Michael Lieber may know, I have benefited the most from those with whom I have had the greatest differences.

I owe very special debts to Leonard Mason (University of Hawaii), Jack Tobin (Majuro, Marshall Islands), and Homer G. Barnett (University of Oregon). Mason guided my initial research efforts with the Bikinians. He has generously made available his own data on the people, and our relationship, both in its professional and personal dimensions, has evolved into one which both my wife and I cherish. Over the past decade, Tobin has willingly shared his substantial knowledge about Marshallese, and he has consistently provided necessary corrections when my notions about the islanders' culture and society strayed off course. Barnett provided my graduate training in anthropology and directed the larger research project on relocated peoples in the Pacific of which this study is but a part. Perhaps more importantly, Barnett shared with his students a vision of what the anthropological endeavor should be.

My greatest indebtedness, of course, is to the Bikinians. They always gave freely of their time and showed a personal interest in and extended a very warm hospitality to my wife and me. For various reasons, I believe that it has been important to describe their community and history. Regrettably, the Bikinians may not like the sections of this study that deal with the competitive dimension of their society, but I have suggested that with respect to this area of their behavior they are—in the last analysis —purely human. Through no fault of their own, they have been a very discontent people since the American occupation of Micronesia, and I hope that their future provides some relief from their more recent past.

University of Minnesota   ROBERT C. KISTE

Contents

Illustrations

PHOTOGRAPHS

MAPS

CHAPTER ONE

Introduction

The People and the Problem

In early 1946 the islanders who inhabited Bikini Atoll in the northern Marshall Islands were relocated from their ancestral homeland because it had been selected as a nuclear test site by the United States. The Bikinians did not desire relocation, but they had no real alternative other than submission to the plans of the Americans.

Bikini is an isolated atoll composed of a number of islands enclosing a large lagoon. The Bikinians had not had extensive contact with outsiders and were among the least Westernized of the Marshallese. They were a self-sufficient people who depended on the outside world for only a few of their wants. Their economy relied heavily upon fishing and the capture of other marine fauna, supplemented by agricultural activities that required a minimal expenditure of time and energy.

Relocation altered almost every facet of the Bikinians' social and physical environments. Their relative isolation from the outside world abruptly ended with their initial resettlement on Rongerik, another northern atoll. Rongerik is much smaller than Bikini, and in less than two years, its resources proved insufficient to support the community. When the islanders suffered from near starvation, they were evacuated and given refuge at a United States military base on Kwajalein Atoll. After several months, they were again resettled, this time on Kili Island in the southern Marshalls. Once on Kili, the Bikinians were faced with the challenge of adapting to an environment quite different from that of Bikini. Kili is not an atoll; rather, it is a single reef island with neither an enclosed lagoon nor a sheltered fishing ground. To gain an adequate subsistence, any population inhabiting Kili would have to make a major commitment to agricultural endeavors.

This study is, in some ways, a history of the Bikini community, but primarily it is an examination of the ways in which the Bikinians have attempted to cope with their relocations. The emphasis is upon the community's social organization and the structure of its relations with its paramount chief and Americans; both have been radically altered in the process of the islanders' attempt to adjust to their relocations and have been crucial variables in determining their successes and failures to adapt to the circumstances which have been imposed upon them.

In a recent survey of Micronesian ethnography, Alkire (1972:38) reviews the work of Mason (1954), Spoehr (1949), and Tobin (1958) and reports that there is agreement ". . . that control of land is a basic theme of Marshallese culture." Control of land may be defined as authority over its disposition and the distribution of products derived from it. In the atoll environment, land is conceived of as a scarce commodity necessary for sustenance, and Marshallese, and perhaps all atoll dwellers, have traditionally considered it their most prized resource. Tobin correctly notes that Marshallese are very competitive when issues pertaining to land are at stake: "People are always plotting to obtain more land" (1958:3).

A facet of Marshallese culture and society which has not been made sufficiently explicit in the literature, however, is that the competition over land represents more than a preoccupation with a particular resource; rather, it is but one manifestation of a larger set of related interests. Marshallese attitudes and behaviors reveal a generalized concern over the distribution and acquisition of power, influence, privilege, and control, not only of land but of all resources which they deem of substantial worth. The concern over these interests is reflected in distinctions in social rank and class which are obtrusive features of the systems of kinship and social organization.[1]

---

[1] It could be argued that a concern over social rank and class and corresponding competition over power and control of resources are not unique

Traditionally, and as the ethnographic literature suggests, the competition has almost invariably been focused on land. [2] The system of landholding and land rights was integrally related to the islanders' lineage and kinship system, and it was the rights to land which defined the most important political and economic relations among individuals and groups. Social statuses entailing authority over land were the supreme prizes in the competitive arena of Marshallese life. Authority over land provided power and influence over others and entitled those who possessed it with special privileges. The statuses were few relative to the aspirants to them, and as a consequence, they were the objects in a never ending rivalry.

Historically, the competition involved both intra- and inter-atoll struggles and warfare. Actual physical conflicts were terminated by colonial powers, but the presence of foreigners has introduced new dimensions to this competition and has altered the means by which traditional ends are pursued. Political statuses which are part of the colonial administrative apparatus have become new prizes employed in familiar struggles. Further, resources from the outside have come to be coveted, and like land, control over these allows for the gratification of material wants and also provides another basis for advantage over others. Thus, novel elements introduced by foreigners have altered the content of Marshallese culture and society, but they have not changed the fundamentally competitive dimension of the islanders' life.

In the case of the Bikinians and consistent with this interpretation of Marshallese culture and society, the strategies and behavioral responses that the islanders have developed in coping with their relocations, and which have resulted in the modification of their own community as well as its relations with the

---

to the Bikinians or Marshallese but that these are common features of most, if not all, Micronesian societies. This thesis has in fact been suggested by McKnight (1960:1-16).

[2] In pre-European times, chiefs also had authority over areas of lagoon and submerged reef which were rich in marine resources. Like land, the control of such areas was competed for by opposing chiefs and their supporters. Colonial governments have terminated chiefly authority and control over marine and lagoon areas declaring them open to all inhabitants of an atoll.

paramount chief and Americans, make it necessary to assume that motivations to gain power, influence, privilege, and control over valued resources are common among them. When these interests are at stake, Bikinians endeavor to manipulate the circumstances of particular situations in ways they perceive as enhancing their own self-interests. Such maneuvers are manifest both in the relations among Bikinians within their own community and in the management of their relations with figures of external power and authority.

Two final points must be made. First, arguing that Bikinians, and Marshallese in general, compete for and manipulate events to gain advantage, does not suggest that they differ from people of other societies. The argument advanced here is in basic agreement with the analyses of a number of anthropologists concerned with the dynamics of social and cultural change who adopt what Schneider (1970:14) has referred to as a "competitive view" of society (also see Leach 1954 and Mair 1965). This view involves the assumptions that people of all societies vie with one another and that the pursuit of power and influence is common to members of human groups either as ends in themselves or as the means of achieving still other goals. In the case of the Bikinians, as with most if not all peoples of the Third World, the attempt to gain influence over the foreign political entity which dominates their lives represents the simple desire to gain some control over their own affairs and destinies.

Secondly and perhaps obviously, while certain objectives are common to Bikinians, it is not assumed nor implied that the intensity of motivation is the same for all individuals or that all are equally successful. As in all societies, some individuals are more aggressive than others in the pursuit of valued ends, and some are inclined to withdraw from the competition for idiosyncratic reasons. Further, some occupy positions in the structure of their society which give them advantage over others, and individuals also differ in their skill in manipulating people and events. Nonetheless, it is those who are the most successful and energetic in the pursuit of power and other goals who chart the direction that a society follows.

Portions of Chapters Three, Five, and Seven give very detailed accounts of the structure of the Bikini community at different times. If this study were concerned about a relatively stable community, such detail could be sacrificed for a description of general patterns. However, in the rapidly changing Bikini community, it is necessary to examine both the exact position that different individuals occupy in their society's structure as well as their various maneuvers to gain advantage. Together, these elements constitute the dynamic processes of change and account for the modifications which have occurred both within the community and in its relations with outsiders.

A Note on the Governing of Men

Chapters One to Eight and the initial section of Chapter Nine are concerned with the Bikinians and to a lesser extent, Marshallese in general. This portion of the book concentrates mainly on anthropological problems about specific facets of the Bikini community and the larger Marshallese society of which it is a part. An attempt has been made to examine as objectively as possible what appears to be not only some of the most salient features of the islanders' culture and behavior, but those which have been major forces of social and cultural change. The point of view which has been adopted for this analysis and the assumptions which underlie it have been made explicit in the foregoing paragraphs. By focusing upon its competitive dimension, however, other facets of the islanders' society have been necessarily neglected, and for a somewhat broader view of Marshallese life, one may wish to refer to Spoehr's description of a village on Majuro Atoll (1949).

The last section of the final chapter is concerned with other issues and is more about Americans than Bikinians or other Marshallese. Here I write not so much as an anthropologist, but as a concerned observer of the United States' presence in Micronesia over the past quarter century with a particular emphasis upon the Marshall Islands. Presented are some reflections about the consequences of American rule in the islands, and a review of some recent developments pertaining to the future of Micronesia. This section reflects certain of my own value positions, and while I believe they are shared by some of my colleagues, they are not to be understood as "facts uncovered by anthropological research." Judgments about what is desirable or undesirable are matters of individual conscience and are not derived from the data of any scientific discipline.

Sources of Data

The Bikinians have graciously tolerated the inquiries of five anthropologists. Initial anthropological work was carried out by researchers serving in applied capacities for the United States Trust Territory of the Pacific Islands because of the difficulties the islanders encountered as a consequence of their resettlements. As a special consultant to the High Commissioner of the Territory, Dr. Leonard Mason (University of Hawaii) surveyed conditions at Rongerik in early 1948. Later in the same year he met with the Bikinians at Kwajalein, and in 1949 he observed the community during a brief stay on Kili. At different times in the early 1950s Dr. Philip Drucker (University of Kentucky) and Dr. Saul H. Riesenberg (Smithsonian Institute) occupied the position of Staff Anthropologist attached to the Office of the High Commissioner. Dr. Drucker produced a substantial report after two months of field research on Kili in 1950. On more than one occasion in 1954, Dr. Riesenberg visited the Bikinians for brief periods and prepared reports for the administration.

The research of Drs. Drucker and Riesenberg overlapped and supplemented the efforts of Dr. Jack A. Tobin. Tobin frequently called at Kili during his tenure as Marshall Islands District Anthropologist from 1950 to 1957, and on two occasions he resided with the community for periods of several weeks. Government records contain a wealth of memoranda and field reports by Dr. Tobin, and each of his periods of residence with the Bikinians resulted in valuable reports.

Dr. Mason renewed his work among the Bikinians during the summer months of 1957 and 1963 as an independent researcher unaffiliated with the Trust Territory administration. On the latter occasion, he introduced my wife and me to the community, and we collaborated in a joint effort from June to August. My wife and I continued work on Kili until February,

1964. Later in the same year, Mason and I again joined forces to interview Bikinians then living at Kwajalein and other atolls in the Marshalls.

In 1967 Dr. Tobin returned to the Marshalls in the capacity of Community Development Advisor and renewed his contacts with the Bikinians. During the summer months of 1969 I returned to Kili for additional work and travelled to Bikini to observe the initial phase of a program which will eventually return the people to their ancestral homeland. A sabbatical leave spent in Honolulu during the academic year 1972-73 and a short trip to the Marshalls in March, 1973 brought me into contact with legal counsels now representing the Bikinians and I learned of some of the most recent events affecting the community.[3]

The data collected by anthropologists are complemented by voluminous government records which extend back to the first visits of Americans to Bikini during the closing months of World War II. Additionally, world press coverage of the Bikinians began when their atoll was first selected as a nuclear test site, and numerous newspaper and magazine articles have appeared in subsequent years. Both government records and published accounts have been useful in filling in the gaps between the research efforts of anthropologists and have provided an independent check as well as different interpretations of events reported by Bikinians.

---

[3] The 1963-64 fieldwork with the Bikinians was conducted within the framework of a larger research effort, *The Project for the Comparative Study of Cultural Change and Stability in Displaced Communities in the Pacific.* The project was directed by Dr. Homer G. Barnett, Department of Anthropology, University of Oregon, and was funded by the National Science Foundation. The 1969 research was made possible by a grant from the Office for International Projects, University of Minnesota.

CHAPTER TWO

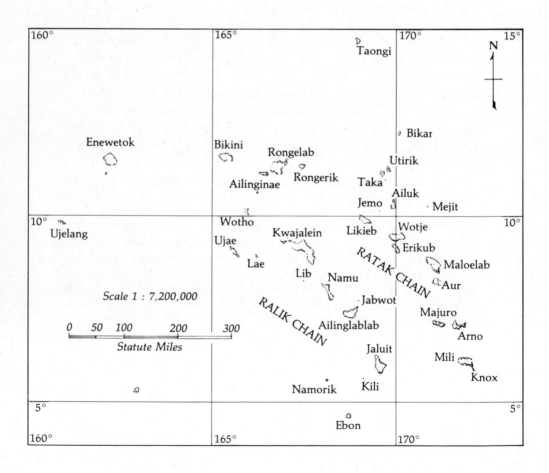

Map 1. The Marshall Islands.

Environmental
and Historical Setting

The Marshall Islands

The Marshall Islands lie on the eastern edge of Micronesia over 2,000 miles southwest of Hawaii in the central Pacific and a few degrees north of the equator (see Map 1). The Marshallese archipelago is composed of twenty-nine atolls and five single islands which are arranged in two roughly parallel chains on a northwest-southeast axis (Bryan 1972:135). The eastern chain is known as Ratak and the western as Ralik. The Marshallese divide the latter into northern and southern seas; Bikini is the northernmost atoll in the northern sea which includes Rongerik Atoll and extends south to include Kwajalein Atoll and Lib Island. Ralik atolls and islands which are located in the latitudes to the south of Lib are in the southern sea; Kili Island is situated in the middle of this southern zone.

All of the Marshalls are formed of coral formations built upward from submerged volcanic peaks, and the discrepancy between land and sea area is one of the most striking features of the environment. The Marshalls are scattered over 375,000 square miles of ocean (an area of about one and one-half the size of Texas) while the total dry land area of all the atolls and islands is slightly less than seventy square miles (about one-twentieth the area of Rhode Island). The elevation of most atolls and islands ranges from eight to twenty feet above low tide level, and there are no high volcanic peaks.

Because of their location in the low latitudes and the absence of large land masses, the Marshalls have a tropical marine climate. Both temperatures (mean annual temperature is 81° F) and humidity (relative humidity averages about 85 percent with little variation) are high and uniform over the archipelago. The islands receive a substantial amount of precipitation, but significant differences in the amount and monthly distribution of rain distinguish the northern from the southern atolls. Bikini and other atolls of the far north have an annual rainfall of approximately sixty inches (Wiens 1962:154). The belt of the northeast trades extends across the northern atolls, and from December to April, the winds blow strong and steady bringing clear skies but little rain. In contrast, the southern atolls receive an annual rainfall about three times greater than that of the north, and as they are situated on the southern margin of the trade-wind belt, rain is more evenly distributed throughout the year. Reflecting the differences in precipitation patterns, the northern atolls have relatively poor soil covers and only three subsistence crops—coconut, pandanus, and arrowroot. The southern atolls have richer soil deposits, a more luxuriant vegetation cover, and the inventory of subsistence crops, in addition to those found in the north, includes breadfruit, taro, papaya, and bananas.

Historically, the sizes of atoll populations have been fairly well correlated with the differences between the ecological conditions of the northern and southern atolls. Generally, the northern atolls have supported relatively small communities. Bikini was typical of the most northern atolls and had only 170 inhabitants in 1946.[1] The largest and densest settlements have always been located in the more favorable environment of the extreme south where some of the atolls have populations of well over 1,000.

The Marshalls and the islands to the west—the Carolines and Marianas—were seized during World War II from Japan which had held them under a League of Nations Mandate. In 1947, with the exception of the island of Guam, the area became the United States Trust Territory of the Pacific Islands within the framework

---

[1] Only 161 islanders were actually resident at Bikini and were moved to Rongerik in 1946; nine others were temporarily absent from the community for reasons of employment, hospitalization, or education.

of the United Nations (see Map 2).[2] Under Article 73 of the
United Nations charter, the United States pledged to ". . . pro-
mote to the utmost the well-being of the inhabitants" while re-
serving the right to establish military sites of strategic value to
its own national security. The Territory was initially governed
by a military government. In 1951, the administration was transferred to the Department of the Interior and civilian control.

In former times European colonial powers had competed
for influence in the area. Traders and missionaries were well
established throughout most of Micronesia by the latter part of
the nineteenth century. A lucrative copra trade created conflict
among Germany, Spain, and England. Germany gained firm control over the Marshalls and declared them a Protectorate in 1885
and thirteen years later, extended its hegemony over the Carolines and most of the Marianas.

Within the Marshalls, Europeans were first attracted to the
more favorable environment and larger populations of the south,
and it was there that trading and mission activities were initiated
in the 1850s. Traders were of several nationalities, but from the
outset German interests were dominant. They taught the islanders to manufacture copra from the meat of the coconut and ex-
changed metal tools and other trade goods for the finished prod-
uct. The missionaries were Americans and Hawaiians dispatched
by the American Board of Commissioners for Foreign Missions.
This nondenominational but mainly Congregational and Presby-
terian Board founded in New England had carried the mission
effort to Hawaii in 1820. Some Catholic priests arrived in the
Marshalls early in the German period, but Catholic influence has
always been limited to a few atolls.

The German colonial government established an administrative headquarters for the Marshalls on Jaluit Atoll some thirty
miles distant from Kili in the southern Ralik sea. The few German administrators accomplished their primary objective of devel-

---

[2] Guam was neither part of the Japanese League of Nations Mandate nor is
it included within the United States Trust Territory of the Pacific Islands.
The island became a possession of the United States in 1898 after the Span-
ish-American War. It was seized by the Japanese early in World War II and
was retaken by American forces in 1944. Guam is the only island in the
Marianas which is not part of the Trust Territory.

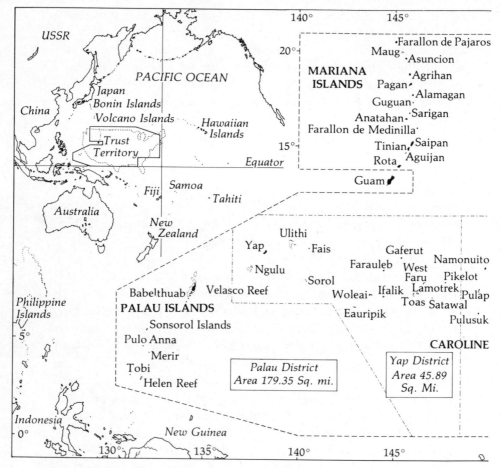

Map 2. The U.S. Trust Territory of the Pacific Islands.

oping the copra trade by working through traditional chiefs who
encouraged islanders to extend their plantings of coconut trees.
With the outbreak of World War I, Japan seized Germany's Micronesian possessions, and large numbers of Japanese officials
and traders further expanded the copra trade and initiated other
economic enterprises, all of which remained in Japanese hands.
A regular shipping schedule was established and maintained between all of the islands, and trading posts were created on a
number of atolls. Jaluit remained the administrative headquarters and became a Japanese center of commerce and culture.

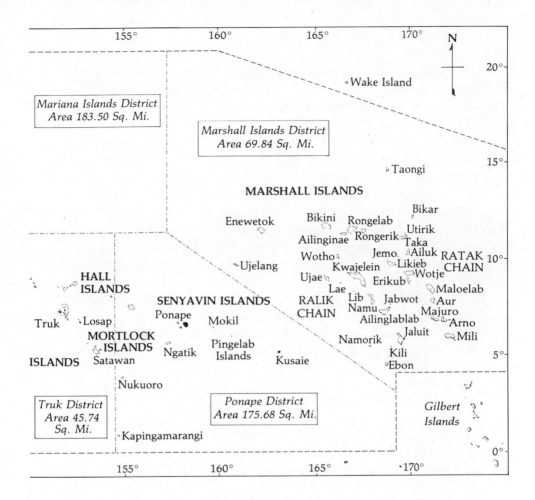

A few schools were created to instruct a limited number of
Marshallese in Japanese traditions and language. Hospitals were
established at Jaluit, Kwajalein, and two other atolls, and for
the first time, some of the islanders received modern medical
treatment for major illnesses. During the latter 1930s and in
the series of events which culminated in World War II, Japan
fortified a number of islands, and their bases on Kwajalein and
Enewetok were among the first in Micronesia to be invaded by
American forces.

Bikini

Bikini is the northernmost atoll in Ralik and relatively distant and isolated from others. Its closest neighbor, Rongelab Atoll, is over eighty miles to the east. Enewetok lies over twice that distance to the west, and Wotho is more than a hundred miles to the south. The largest of Bikini's twenty-six islands covers 0.66 square miles; it and the other twenty-five have a combined land area of 2.32 square miles. The reef upon which the islands are built encloses a lagoon area of approximately 243 square miles. The lagoon is roughly oval, some twenty-six miles long, and has a maximum width of about fifteen miles (see Map 3). A large pass in the southeastern section of the reef provides a channel easily negotiated by large ocean-going vessels.

Legendary accounts and genealogical records give evidence that the Bikinians were descended from a group of islanders who fled Wotje Atoll in the Ratak chain in the not too distant past. According to legend, a man named Larkelon who belonged to a chiefly line of the Ijjirik matriclan at Wotje was forced to flee the atoll after a dispute. He and a group of followers from his own clan and that of Makaoliej sailed to the Ralik chain arriving at Bikini which was purportedly inhabited by a small number of people. Larkelon is said to have threatened to make war upon them, and they are held to have taken to their canoes in fright and sailed away never to be seen again (Mason 1954:21-22; Tobin 1953:2-4).

While the legend cannot be taken as historically accurate, it is of sociological significance. Larkelon established himself as *iroij* 'chief' of Bikini, and his matrilineal descendants succeeded him. As the chiefly genealogy was remembered, the chief of the community in 1946, known as Juda, was a member of the fifth descending generation from Larkelon.

Although it is not certain when Larkelon's group arrived at Bikini, historical evidence when combined with the genealogical record suggests that the event occurred before 1800. It is certain, however, that the descendants of Larkelon's group were relatively few and had little contact with outsiders up to and including early European times. The Bikinians occasionally

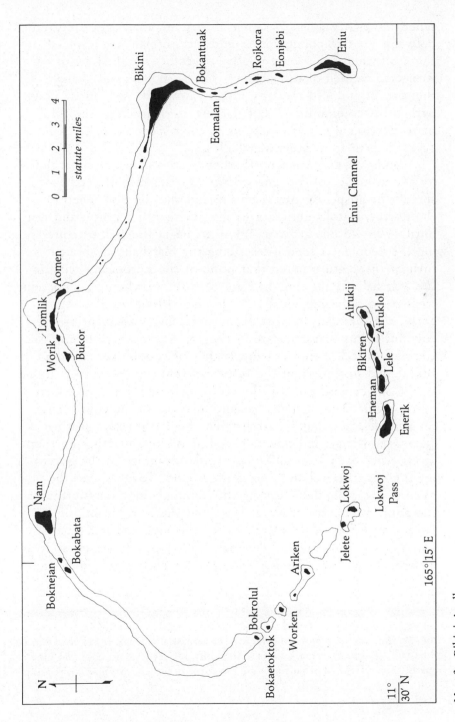

Map 3. Bikini Atoll.

sailed the eighty miles to Rongelab. A few marriages occurred between the two communities, and a third clan was founded on the atoll when Larkelon's chiefly successors acquired a pair of Rongelab women of the Rinamu clan as spouses and brought them to Bikini. No regular contacts, however, were maintained with other communities. Left largely to themselves, the Bikinians developed minor variations in their speech which distinguished them from other Marshallese.

Bikinians and other northerners were the last to be affected by the influence of foreigners. Native evangelists trained to spread the gospel by American missionaries did not penetrate the northern atolls until late in the nineteenth century, and not until 1908 did one arrive at Bikini to begin the task of converting the people. A report describing the Marshalls at about the turn of the century noted that none of the Europeans living in the Marshalls at the time had yet seen Bikini where ". . . coconut trees stand only individually." (Jeschke 1906:272-3)[3] Apparently, the Bikinians did not begin increasing their plantings of coconut palms to participate in the copra trade until late in the German period. Few German officials or vessels ever called at Bikini, and not many of the Bikinians ventured away from home.

Contact with the outside world increased during the Japanese period. The islanders became involved in the copra trade on a modest scale, and a government field trip vessel bearing Japanese officials and traders called at Bikini and other northern atolls twice each year. Bikinians took advantage of the government ships to travel and ceased their canoe voyages over the open sea to Rongelab. During this time, about three-fourths of the adult population made at least one trip away from home. Several males worked as laborers for the Japanese at Kwajalein and Jaluit, a few sailed as deckhands on Japanese vessels and two attended Japanese schools. The most adventuresome man trav-

---

[3] Bikini had been discovered in 1824 by the Russian explorer Otto von Kotzebue. The atoll was visited in 1858 by another Russian, Chramtschenko. By the time of the German Protectorate, several European vessels had visited the atoll. Jeschke's remarks apparently only reflect that none of the Europeans living in the Marshalls around the turn of the century had visited Bikini.

elled as far south as the southern Ratak chain and was also employed for a time on Kili, then a copra plantation. A few men
and women journeyed to Kwajalein to take advantage of its medical facilities, and others travelled abroad simply for adventure.
A small number found spouses on other atolls and established
residences away from Bikini.

Most Bikinians who ventured beyond Bikini's reef, however,
confined their travels to brief excursions within the northern
atolls. Journeys away from the home community, while no
doubt exciting, were not always pleasurable. The more acculturated Marshallese considered the Bikinians to be a backward people.
They compared them with their own ancestors of pre-European
times and found the peculiarities in their speech humorous. The
Bikinians had accepted this unflattering image and held themselves
in rather low esteem. To a certain extent, they did not identify
with other Marshallese, but thought of themselves as "Bikinians,"
a people distinct and culturally inferior. Most found it more
comfortable to remain at home (Mason 1954:27-33; Richard
1957:507).

Not until World War II did foreigners come to reside at Bikini. A small unit of five Japanese soldiers established a weather
station on the atoll. Bikinians were convinced that Japan was
the most powerful nation in the world, and this belief was affirmed by the soldiers who told of Japan's exploits at war. Apparently, the islanders did not resist when these soldiers imposed
a strict regimen, conscripted their labor, established curfews, and
suspended Christian services. With the American invasion of the
Marshalls, the Bikinians' image of the Japanese was shattered.
The Japanese soldiers committed suicide rather than confront
the small unit of American troops which arrived at Bikini on
March 29, 1944. The Americans assured the islanders that they
had nothing to fear, and they turned over all Japanese food supplies and some equipment to them. The initial impression made
by the Americans was thus quite favorable. The Bikinians were
glad to be rid of the strict military rule, and the Americans' gen-
erosity with the Japanese food stocks (2,500 pounds of rice and
substantial quantities of canned meat and fish) represented a
small bonanza.

The Paramount Chief

The factors of geography and environment which impeded the spread of European influence to the northern atolls also accounted for the fact that Bikini had remained outside the domain of any *iroij lablab* 'paramount chief' until European times. In the pre-contact era, most of the atolls in the Marshalls were divided among the realms of several paramount chiefs. Each of the chiefs was the head of a chiefly matrilineage, and he and his lineage mates comprised the highest ranking strata of a privileged social class. (The class system is best described by Mason 1947.) The amount of power and influence possessed by a paramount chief was in direct proportion to the number of atolls and islands in his domain and the number of *kajur* under his authority. *Kajur* was the class of commoners to which the majority of islanders belonged, and the term also denoted the power or strength of a chief.

A paramount chief maintained control over his realm by his success and reputation as a war leader. The several chiefs warred against one another as each attempted to extend his domain, and conflicts within the same chiefly lineage were commonplace. The extent of the respective domains of the several chiefs varied constantly with the fortunes of war.[4]

About 1870 a certain Kabua came into power after conflict had divided a chiefly lineage, and by conquest he began to extend his domain in the Ralik chain. Apparently, it was shortly thereafter that he sent a subordinate to Bikini with a force of men. Kabua was described as a powerful chieftain, and without the use of force, the Bikinians were persuaded to acknowledge his sovereignty over them. All Bikinians, including their own chief, became Kabua's subjects, and thereafter they were obligated to render tribute in the form of finely woven pandanus leaf mats, coconut fiber sennit, and preserved foodstuffs and were required to

---

[4] Prowess as a warrior also provided a means of upward mobility for males of the commoner class. Men who distinguished themselves in battle were rewarded with land, and sometimes they were appointed to oversee portions of a paramount chief's domain. A good account of warfare in the southern Ratak has recently been provided by Rynkiewich (1972).

send domestics to serve in one of his several households. Kabua was expected to reciprocate by sending them occasional gifts of food from the south, and it was his obligation to protect them and provide aid in times of disaster from storms or other calamities.

After the Germans established their Protectorate, the colonial government with the support of the missionaries imposed an end to island warfare. The chiefs were given formal recognition and were made the legal owners of the islands and atolls within their respective domains as they existed at that point in time. Subsequently, and with the one exception noted below, the Japanese and American governments have respected the legitimacy of the arrangement. The rights and obligations of the paramount chiefs were defined by the Germans and Japanese. They were guaranteed a percentage of the copra from their lands and were required to pay taxes levied on their subjects. Under the Japanese, the chiefs were also made responsible for medical expenses incurred by their subjects.

Toward the end of the Japanese era, the small contingent of Japanese soldiers stationed at Bikini challenged the rights of Kabua's successors to the atoll. They informed the Bikinians that the rights of the paramount chief had been preempted by the Japanese Emperor and that the atoll and its resources were his possession to be used in support of the weather station. The claim was not otherwise legitimized, but it was to become a factor of some significance after the American occupation of the islands. From the outset of its administration, the United States, while recognizing the paramount chiefs as the legitimate owners of their respective domains, has pursued a laissez-faire policy pertaining to chiefs' relations with their subjects. The chiefs have not been held responsible for taxes, and the rights and obligations between chiefs and commoners have been considered a matter of traditional Marshallese custom and have been left to the islanders.

Historically, Bikini was never very important to Kabua or to his successors who had their residences in the more southern atolls. In Japanese times a half-dozen Bikinians travelled south to Ailinglablab Atoll to serve as domestics in the chiefly household located there. Otherwise, Bikini's isolation and distance from the south, its small population, the paucity of its resources, and the small quantity of copra produced on the atoll made it of negligible value to the chiefs, and they seldom visited there. All communication between the paramount chief and the Bikinians was severed during the war years. After the Americans' arrival, the chief made one visit to Bikini as a passenger on a navy vessel; on that occasion, the Bikinians offered the traditional tribute, and the chief reciprocated with a small gift of imported food (Mason 1954:491).

The Years 1944 and 1945

With the advent of the American Naval Military Government, the Bikinians received more attention from the foreign power which dominated the islands than they had ever experienced in the past. American field trip vessels visited the northern atolls every two or three months. Members of the American field trip parties included a medical officer who rendered free medical treatment and an officer in charge of economic affairs. The latter encouraged the islanders to resume the production of copra and to produce handicraft items; these found a ready market at Kwajalein which had become a major military base in support of the American push into the western Pacific.

The military government introduced several innovations during 1944 and 1945. As part of the administration's Territory-wide health and welfare program, a modest store, an elementary school, and a medical dispensary were established on the atoll; each was staffed by a Bikinian who was taken to Kwajalein for training by navy personnel.

At the Americans' suggestion, the eleven traditional leaders of the community, who were known as *alab,* formed a council which functioned as the governing body of the community. According to the Americans' design, the council was headed by a magistrate, known in Marshallese as *ritil ailing* 'one who leads the island'. Juda, the hereditary chief and descendant of the legendary Larkelon, was among the eleven leaders, and he was named by them to be magistrate.

Aside from the innovations introduced by the Americans and the greater frequency of contact with the outside world, the period immediately after the war witnessed a return to the more traditional life style which had been interrupted by the Japanese

military. All of the islanders had their permanent dwellings on
Bikini Island, and daily life was rather relaxed and without rigid
routine. Women's activities centered around the residence units,
domestic chores, and the rearing of children. Men were primarily
occupied with the collection of subsistence crops, fishing, and the
maintenance and construction of canoes and dwellings.

The islanders' economy was based on a minimal agricultural
effort and extensive exploitation of marine resources. Their three
crops were well adapted to the northern atolls; none required
much care, and the people had a very casual attitude toward
agricultural endeavors. Seed coconuts were simply planted in
shallow holes and left untended. Pandanus was propagated by
cuttings from mature trees and required little further care. After
arrowroot was excavated with a simple digging stick, a future
crop was ensured by the few tubers left in the ground.

The starch extracted from the small arrowroot tubers was
of minor significance; the pandanus and coconut were the most
important crops. The pandanus tree produced a seasonal fruit
of substantial nutritional value which was consumed raw or processed into a dried paste and stored against lean times. Coconuts
provided an edible meat, the only cash crop, and a thirst-quench-
ing liquid. The latter was especially important as fresh water was
periodically scarce in the relatively dry zone of the north. The
Bikinians collected rain water in a few cisterns which ran dry during the winter period of the northeast trades. Slightly brackish
water was available from wells on the largest islands of the atoll,
but it was less potable than the cistern water. The people preferred and depended upon the coconut.

The people kept a few pigs and chickens and sometimes
caught wild sea birds and land crabs. None of these sources of
protein contributed substantially to the diet; the pigs and chickens were reserved for special occasions. The islanders' attitudes
towards animal husbandry were similar to those evidenced in
their agricultural endeavors. Both pigs and chickens were usually
allowed to run free and to fend for themselves.

With their small inventory of plants and animals, the Bikinians had the essentials of life, but they enjoyed little surplus.
The few coconuts that they could spare were processed into
copra and sold to obtain cloth for clothing and canoe sails, fish-

hooks, tools, utensils, kerosene lamps, small quantities of rice, flour, tea, coffee, sugar, and occasional cans of meat or fish. Other trade goods were rare, and the people manufactured most items in their material culture from local resources. They produced a large variety of baskets from coconut fronds. Fiber from coconut husks was the raw material for a high quality sennit that was used in house and canoe construction. Pandanus leaf was processed into mats and thatch panels for house roofs and walls. A limited number of hardwoods was available for house frames, canoes, and bowls.

Outrigger canoes played an important part in Bikini life and allowed the people to be very mobile within the atoll. The outriggers were of two types. In 1946, eight of the Bikinians' canoes were sailing vessels with hulls approaching thirty feet in length and lateen sails rigged on twenty-foot masts. The sailing canoes required a crew of two or three men and could transport a sizeable load of cargo and as many as seven or eight passengers. The large canoes were used for travel within the lagoon, and in contrast to earlier times, they were less frequently employed in the open sea. The seven small one-man paddle canoes were less important and were used off the shore of the main island but were not designed for sailing or lagoon crossings.

Men employed both types of canoes to exploit Bikini's abundant marine resources upon which the people were so reliant. Large deep-water game fish such as tuna and bonito were caught by trolling the lagoon and ocean waters in the sailing canoes. Men also sailed to distant points in the atoll where schools of lagoon fish were caught by the surround method and by spear fishing. Turtles and shellfish were also collected during such ventures. Of less importance was the drop-line method of fishing with a weighted line from the small paddle canoes.

The sailing canoes were also used to collect subsistence crops. Families often sailed from the large island to their landholdings on other islands within the atoll where they remained for several days collecting and processing their crops. The people greatly enjoyed such expeditions as they served to break the monotony of life on the main island and provided an opportunity to find relief from their fellows with whom they had daily face-to-face contact. Sailing the lagoon's waters was in itself a form

Plate 1. Outrigger sailing canoe with Bikini Island in background, 1946. *(Photo by Carl Mydans. Time-Life, Inc.)*

Plate 2. Outrigger sailing canoe similar to those used by the Bikinians prior to their relocation. The outrigger in foreground is being loaded with copra bags. (The canoes are those of the Enewetok people on Ujelang Atoll.) *(Photo by author.)*

of recreation. Men sometimes sailed simply for sport, and fishing
expeditions were seldom devoted entirely to work. Men took
pleasure in their fishing ventures, often stopping at small islands
to refresh themselves with coconut and to explore for driftwood
and other objects cast up by the sea.

Men devoted a considerable amount of time and energy to
constructing and maintaining their canoes. They fashioned hulls
from hand-shaped planks which were lashed together with sennit.
Maintenance was a never-ending task as canoes frequently required
caulking, renewal of sennit lashings, and replacement of broken or
deteriorated planks. Men took great pride in their canoes; a craft
that was swift and easily maneuverable was especially prized (Kiste
1972:80-82).

All economic activity was suspended on Sundays. The most
routinized aspects of Bikinian life were the consequences of mission effort. By 1946, the islanders' version of the fundamental-
istic Protestantism derived from New England had become firmly
established as an integral part of their culture. (Spoehr's description of the mixture of traditional and Christian beliefs and the
organization of the church at Majuro is fairly representative of the
entire Marshalls [1949:221-31].) The pastor of the church was a
Bikini man who had been trained by the missionaries. The community celebrated all Protestant holidays. The Sabbath was observed with both morning and afternoon services and a strict pro-
hibition on work and most recreation. Two afternoon services
marked the weekly calendar, and elders of the church met on
the first of each month to conduct church business and to plan
services for the coming month.

Initial Relocation

The detonation of atomic bombs over Hiroshima and Naga-
saki in 1945 had ended the war in the Pacific and ushered the
world into the Atomic Age. The nature and effects of the destructive force that had outmoded earlier concepts of warfare
were, however, little known or understood, and the future role
of nuclear weapons in the arsenal of the United States was undetermined. In the weeks following the war, American military

and political leaders began planning nuclear experiments to gather
military and scientific knowledge. Attention soon focused on the
question of the effects of nuclear weapons employed against naval
vessels (Hines 1962:21). A pair of tests given the code name of
Operation Crossroads was planned, and in November of 1945 a
search for an appropriate site began.[5] It had to be located in an
area controlled by the United States and was to be uninhabited
or have a small population which could be easily relocated. The
site had to be in a climatic zone free from storms and cold temperatures, and have a large and sheltered anchorage for a fleet of
target vessels. The danger of radioactive contamination required
a site distant from heavily populated areas and at least 500 miles
from all sea and air routes. In late January, 1946, navy officials
in Washington, D.C. announced that Bikini Atoll fulfilled all climatic and geographical conditions for Operation Crossroads. Ironically, some of the same factors of geography and environment
which had limited the Bikinians' contact with the outside world
caused an abrupt end to their isolation and thrust them into the
mainstream of events of the twentieth century. Further, the
Christianity which the islanders had accepted from Americans
was employed to convince them of the necessity of their relocation.

The Bikinians' initial relocation was accomplished swiftly
and with little planning. The military governor of the Marshalls
obtained the consent of the Bikinians' paramount chief to move
his subjects. On Sunday, February 10, 1946 the governor, members of his staff, and the paramount chief arrived at Bikini by
seaplane. After the morning church services had been concluded,
the Bikinians were addressed by the governor. According to his
own account, he drew upon the Bible and:

> . . . compared the Bikinians to the children of Israel whom the Lord
> saved from their enemy and led unto the Promised Land. He told
> them of the bomb that men in America had made and the destruc-
> tion it had wrought upon the enemy (Richard 1957:510).

---

[5] After Operation Crossroads in 1946, Bikini was not utilized as a nuclear
test site for eight years. In 1954, further tests were conducted at the atoll,
and the last occurred in 1958 (Hines 1962:157-195; 270-292).

He further explained that scientists were experimenting with
nuclear devices ". . .for the good of mankind and to end all
world wars" and told how the navy had searched the world for
a test site and had determined that Bikini was the best (ibid.).

The Bikinians deliberated, and according to the governor's
description of events, chief Juda reported their decision:

> If the United States government and the scientists of the world want
> to use our island and atoll for furthering development, which with
> God's blessing will result in kindness and benefit to all mankind, my
> people will be pleased to go elsewhere (Mason 1954:263).

While official sources report that the Bikinians agreed to relocate for the good of all humanity, it is more likely that other
factors were critical in shaping their decision. The islanders were
accustomed to authority imposed from the outside (the paramount chief and the colonial governments which preceded that
of the Americans), and in 1946, they were still impressed by the
United States' decisive defeat of Japan. The Americans' description of their nuclear weapons further convinced them of the
power and technological superiority of the United States, and
when they were requested to give up their ancestral homeland
by both the Americans and their paramount chief, it is doubtful
that they believed that they had any alternative but to comply.

It is not certain whether the problem of selecting a site for
the resettlement of the community was discussed during the governor's visit to Bikini. An official report of the relocation simply
indicates: "Of the eleven family heads (*alab*), nine named Rongerik Atoll as their first choice for the resettlement" (Meade 1946).
There were several factors which appeared to determine the Bikinians' selection of Rongerik. First, the islanders were familiar
with the atoll since it is only eighteen miles from Rongelab whose
people the Bikinians had long been in contact (see Map 1). Second, Rongerik was uninhabited, and resettlement there offered
the promise that the Bikinians could continue their lives free from
the interference of outsiders. Lastly, there is some evidence which
indicates that the Bikinians were never convinced that their relocation was more than a temporary measure, and as a result, they may
not have considered the selection of a new home site to be an important matter.

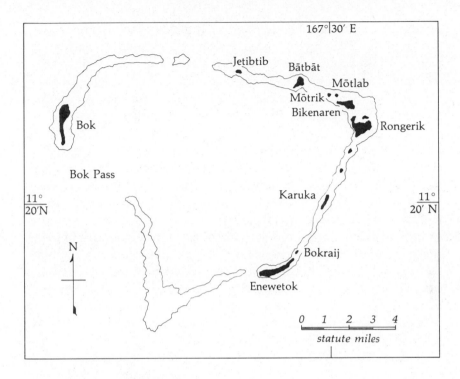

167°|30′ E

Jetibtib   Bātbāt

Mōtlab

Mōtrik

Bikenaren

Bok   Rongerik

Bok Pass

11°
20′N

Karuka

11°
20′ N

N

Bokraij

Enewetok

0   1   2   3   4

statute miles

Map 4. Rongerik Atoll.

Surveys of Rongerik by navy personnel revealed that it
might present some problems of economic self-sufficiency for
the community. The atoll is much smaller than Bikini. In contrast to Bikini's twenty-six islands and land area of 2.32 square
miles, Rongerik has only ten islands with a total area of about
0.63 square miles; the largest of the ten islands covers a scant
0.17 square miles as opposed to the 0.66 square miles of Bikini
Island. Rongerik's lagoon of fifty-five square miles is less than
one-fourth that of Bikini's (see Map 4). Further, as Rongerik
was only occasionally visited by the people of Rongelab, it was
not developed to support a permanent population of any size,
and the quality and quantity of its subsistence crops were not
impressive (Mason 1954:264).
    The administration sought the counsel of the Bikinians'
paramount chief. He urged that the people be moved to either
Ujae or Lae Atolls in northern Ralik; both were inhabited and

were included within his domain.[6] The chief was strongly opposed to the Bikinians' choice of Rongerik; it and Rongelab were
part of the realm of another paramount chief. Aerial and sea
reconnaissance by navy officials eliminated Ujae because of navi-
gational and beaching facilities, and Lae was considered too small
to support both its own inhabitants and the Bikinians.[7]

By February 23, officials announced that they judged Rongerik the best of the three alternatives. That same day, an LST
arrived at Bikini laden with supplies required to build a new village.[8] The provisions included canvas, prefabricated tent frames,
wooden floor platforms, lumber, cement, corrugated metal roofing for water catchment, carpentry and masonry tools, 30,000
gallons of fresh water, and a food supply for the community. At
the instruction of the Americans, the Bikinians dismantled their
church and council house (both were well-built structures considered worthy of removal) and prepared large quantities of pandanus leaf thatch for transport to Rongerik. An advance party
of twenty-two Bikini men and fifteen Seabees boarded the vessel, and it departed on the evening of the day it arrived.

Rongerik was reached the following day. The advance party
cleared land on the main island for a village and erected the tent
frames. Within eight days, the military government officer in
charge of the operation reported that the ". . . essential construc-

---

[6] Ujae Atoll has fourteen islands with a total land area of 0.72 square miles;
its lagoon area is about 72 square miles. In 1946, its population numbered
slightly over 120 people. Lae Atoll has seventeen islands with a total land
area of 0.56 square miles and a small lagoon of less than 7 square miles. In
1946, its population was about 100 (Bryan 1972:142-143; Mason 1954:265).

[7] The naval historian, Commander Dorothy E. Richard, indicates that Wotho
Atoll was also recommended by the paramount chief at this time as another
possibility for resettlement. Richard also reports that several Bikinians were
flown to Wotho, Ujae, and Lae to inspect the atolls (1957:511). The official report by the military government officer in charge of the relocation,
however, makes no mention of Wotho nor does it indicate that any of the
Bikinians were given the opportunity to inspect the sites proposed for initial
resettlement (Meade 1946). Richard confused the events surrounding the
Rongerik relocation with those of a later date.

[8] An LST is a naval craft specially designed for putting ashore troops and
equipment.

tion of the village was complete" (Meade 1946). On March 5 the LST started out for Bikini leaving a skeleton work force on Rongerik to apply canvas to the tent frames and to construct concrete cisterns.

As preparations were being made for the islanders' relocation, ships began entering the Bikini lagoon to launch Operation Crossroads. The operation was a military-scientific program of a magnitude which had no precedent. About 250 vessels (70 of which became target ships), more than 150 aircraft for transport, liaison, and observation, and some 42,000 military, scientific, and technical personnel and observers were eventually involved. Unquestionably, the operation was the most thoroughly documented reported, and publicized peacetime military exercise in history. The official records fill volumes, and coverage by the press was authorized by the President of the United States. Such concentration of attention in addition to the sheer magnitude of the operation gave Crossroads the quality of the spectacular (Hines 1962:31-32).

The Navy Hydrographic Office survey ships *Sumner* and *Bowditch* were among the first to arrive. Their crews consisted of oceanographers, geologists, botanists, biologists, and engineers. These specialists conducted surveys of the islands, reef, and lagoon, catalogued and classified the flora and fauna, and blasted a deep water channel through the reef to the beach on the main island to facilitate the passage of various landing craft.

As more vessels arrived, the tempo of preparatory activities increased, and the Bikinians were overwhelmed by all that they observed. Most of the islanders received their first introduction to motion pictures while waiting for relocation. Each evening, movies were shown on the afterdeck of the *Sumner*. While it is certain that they understood little of what they saw, they were reported completely engrossed with such films as a Roy Rogers western, a Hollywood bedroom farce, and Mickey Mouse in technicolor (Markwith 1946:108).

A great amount of publicity and fanfare was focused upon the Bikinians. Much to the displeasure of the paramount chief, Juda became known in the American press as "King Juda of Bikini." Commercial newsreel teams arrived at the atoll during the last week of February, and by the time a navy photographic

team from Washington, D.C. arrived on March 2, the Bikinians
had learned the meaning of the motion picture camera and were
enjoying the novelty of posing for photographers. On Sunday,
March 3, photographers recorded the last church service performed
on Bikini, and the islanders cooperated by repeating the service
three times before the camera men were satisfied. One of them
later commented that the people were in the process of becoming movie actors:

> The young girls were especially susceptible and giggled and posed as
> soon as a lens was turned their way. However, by the third day of
> our stay, there were so many photographers around, all shooting at
> once, that the girls hardly knew whom to pose for. As soon as one
> of the professionals settled on an angle, several of the amateurs fell
> in around him, and after much discussion of exposure, film speed,
> etc., there was a fusillade of shutter clicks (Markwith 1946:109):

Apparently, the military government had originally planned
to move the Bikinians on March 6, but the demands of the news
agencies and navy photographic team caused a one day delay in
the loading of the LST which had returned from Rongerik. The
military governor's February 10th visit to Bikini and his negoti-

Plate 3. Last church service on Bikini, 1946. *(World Wide Photos.)*

ations with the people were re-enacted for the photgraphers. The
community's cemetery was cleaned and decorated with flowers
and palm fronds, and a ceremony was held to bid farewell to the
Bikinians' ancestors and to entrust their souls to the care of God.
The purpose of the ceremony was marred when the camera-con-
scious Bikinians vied for positions immediately in front of the
cameras, and it was necessary to repeat the performance for a
second filming (see photographs in Markwith's article in the *National Geographic Magazine* July, 1946).

   By the afternoon of March 7, the islanders had loaded their
personal possessions, nearly one ton of pandanus thatch panels,
and canoes on board the LST. They crowded the rails of the
main deck as the vessel departed Bikini's lagoon. Some sang
songs of farewell. Most were silent; some wept (Mason 1954:
276). A photographer who accompanied the Bikinians on their

Plate 4. Bikinians loading their personal possessions aboard LST 1108 for
the move to Rongerik, 1946. *(Photo by Carl Mydans. Time-Life, Inc.)*

overnight voyage to Rongerik provided the first documentary evidence that they considered their relocation to be a temporary inconvenience; he was informed by the islanders "... that they would come back to Bikini someday" (*Life Magazine* 20:105-109, March 25, 1946).

The Bikinians arrived at Rongerik on March 8, 1946. Less than a month had elapsed since the date they had first learned of their impending relocation.

CHAPTER THREE

Bikini
Social Organization

In order to examine the changes which have occurred within the Bikini community as a consequence of its relocations, it is necessary to consider its social organization prior to 1946. This chapter describes the islanders' clan, lineage, and kinship organizations and their system of land tenure, emphasizing throughout rights to land. The islanders' identity as "Bikinians" was largely derived from the fact that they possessed rights to Bikini's twenty-six islands and held those rights because their ancestors had conquered the atoll. Further, the social order of their community was primarily defined and structured by rights to land as they had been inherited from previous generations.

Clans and Lineages

The Marshallese clan is a social category composed of matri-lineages bearing a common name. Lineages belonging to the same clan are scattered throughout the islands and are thought to be related, but in most instances, actual genealogical connections are unknown. Most clans are exogamous and are a medium for the provision of hospitality; islanders are obliged to provide food and shelter for a fellow clansman, whether he is a stranger or a friend.[1]

---

[1] Exceptions to the rule of clan exogamy are known to occur on Arno Atoll in the southern Ratak; an examination of the factors accounting for these exceptions will appear elsewhere (Kiste and Rynkiewich, forthcoming).

The matrilineages composing the clans are unilineal descent units known as *bwij*. Individuals automatically become members of their mother's *bwij* at birth and membership is unalterable. The *bwij* is a highly segmented genealogical structure. All individuals who can trace descent through females from a known female ancestress belong to her *bwij*. Her daughters are the progenitors of *bwij* of a lower order, and *bwij* of ever diminishing genealogical depth occur as the females of each successive generation bear children. A female with a child constitutes the smallest unit which may be termed a *bwij*. The *bwij* are not named, but any particular one, or segment thereof, may be designated by reference to its founder, for example, *bwij in Lakabwit* denotes 'lineage of Lakabwit'.

Most Bikinians belonged to one of the three main clans on their atoll: Ijjirik, Makaoliej, and Rinamu. Each clan was represented by one large *bwij* which may be considered a sub-clan within the overall clan organization of the Marshalls. Branches of the sub-clan were landholding corporations which may be called lineages, and branches of the lineage corporations may be referred to as lineage segments.

The members of a sub-clan were ranked according to two principles: relative chronological age and seniority of generation. The first was expressed in the relations among siblings. Members of a sibling set were ranked from eldest to youngest. As an extension of the same principle, the lineages of a sub-clan were ranked according to the relative ages of the sisters who founded them, and lineage segments were ordered in a similar manner. The second principle was equally simple: ascending generations within a sub-clan, lineage, or lineage segment were superior in rank to descending generations.

Unilineal descent groups which allow no alterations in their memberships inevitably fluctuate considerably in size, and matrilineages such as those found in the Marshalls and elsewhere in Micronesia readily double or halve their membership in the space of one or two generations (Goodenough 1955:80). That is, as a consequence of the differential fertility rates of females at any given time, there are always some lineages which are developing new segments and expanding in size while others are contracting and becoming extinct. This process may be observed by examining the demographic structure of the Bikini community and the composition of its sub-clans and their constituent lineages.

In the decades prior to relocation, the community had been expanding in size. The first accurate census data are from the Japanese period, and as Table 3.1 indicates, earlier population figures are only estimates. The last account from the German period suggests a population of about eighty for the early part of the century. Genealogical data indicate that while this figure may be somewhat low, it is approximately correct. From all of the data assembled in Table 3.1 it appears that the population had begun to increase sometime before the turn of the century and had doubled in size between 1900 and 1946.

As the population had expanded, each sub-clan had increased

Table 3.1. Bikini Community, Population Data: 1862–1973[a]

Year	Number of individuals comprising the community	Number of islanders related to the community but resident elsewhere
1862	50	?
1880s	30	?
1906	"a few families"	?
1913	80	?
1930	127	?
1946	170	48
1953	191	?
1964	282	177
1969	344	196
1973	400+	?

[a] All population figures prior to 1930 are estimates made by sea captains or German travellers and/or officials. The 1930 data were reported in a census conducted by the Japanese government. The 1946 figures are derived from United States Naval Military Government records. The 1953 data were reported by Tobin (1953:52). The 1964 and 1969 data are based on the author's census. The 1973 figure was reported by Tobin (personal communication).

numerically, but their rates of expansion were quite unequal, and
large disparities in size had developed among the lineages of each
sub-clan. Prior to the surge in population, Ijjirik and Makaoliej
were roughly equal in size while Rinamu was much smaller, reflecting its recent arrival on the atoll. As Tables 3.2, 3.3, and 3.4 indicate, by 1946 Makaoliej had outstripped the other two sub-clans,
accounting for a little more than half of all Bikini clansmen.

Figures 1, 2, and 3 portray the genealogies of the sub-clans
and reflect the changes which had occurred in their demographic
structures. For each of the sub-clans, the generation to which
most married adults belonged in 1946 is designated as G^0. Ascending generations are progressively numbered G^{+1}, G^{+2}, etc.;
similarly, the first descending generation is numbered G^{-1}.

As Figure 1 shows, Ijjirik clansmen were descendants of a
female named Lakabwit of the G^{+3} generation. Three of her offspring were females of child-bearing age during the latter third of
the nineteenth century; each founded a branch of Ijjirik, and its
expansion began with their children. By 1946, each of the three
branches was a corporate lineage: the eldest daughter was the progenitor of the senior lineage (I 1); the second eldest founded the

Table 3.2. Composition of the Bikini Community by Clan

Clan	1946 Sex	Total	1964 Sex	Total	1969 Sex	Total
Ijjirik	22 m 29 f	51	46 m 49 f	95	47 m 64 f	111
Makaoliej	37 m 51 f	88	61 m 61 f	122	69 m 73 f	142
Rinamu	13 m 12 f	25	18 m 28 f	46	24 m 33 f	57
Subtotal	72 m 92 f	164	125 m 138 f	263	140 m 170 f	310
Other clans	4 m 2 f	6	7 m 12 f	19	19 m 15 f	34
Total	76 m 94 f	170	132 m 150 f	282	159 m 185 f	344

Table 3.3. Bikini Clansmen and Relatives
not Resident within the Community

Clan	1946		1964		1969	
	Sex	Total	Sex	Total	Sex	Total
Ijjirik	10 m 4 f	14	9 m 3 f	12	9 m 3 f	12
Makaoliej	11 m 9 f	20	32 m 28 f	60	34 m 38 f	72
Rinamu	1 m 0 f	1	4 m 8 f	12	6 m 3 f	9
Subtotal	22 m 13 f	35	45 m 39 f	84	49 m 44 f	93
Other clans	5 m 8 f	13	45 m 48 f	93	46 m 57 f	103
Total	27 m 21 f	48	90 m 87 f	177	95 m 101 f	196

second ranking lineage (I 2); and the junior lineage (I 3) was descended from the youngest of Lakabwit's offspring. Most of Ijjirik's expansion had occurred in the junior lineage. The senior
and second ranking lineages had never been large, and in 1946
it was evident that both were faced with extinction. The senior
lineage had only three members left and the second had five; the
females of both were either aged or infertile. In contrast, the
junior lineage had a membership of fifty-seven.

Figure 2 indicates even more striking imbalances in the demographic structure of Makaoliej. A senior lineage (M 1) had become extinct early in the century, and the second ranking lineage
(M 2) thus assumed senior rank. This lineage had never had more
than a few members, and by 1946 it was represented by a single
male. As in the case of Ijjirik, Makaoliej's expansion had occurred in the junior line of descent (M 3); its G^{+1} females were
quite prolific, and the junior line had developed two sizeable
branches and one small branch. The senior of these (M 3/1) had
forty-four members and was a corporate lineage. The next ranking branch (M 3/2) had fifty-nine members, while the one of jun-

Table 3.4. Total Number of Bikini Clansmen and Relatives

Clan	1946 Sex	Total	1964 Sex	Total	1969 Sex	Total
Ijjirik	32 m 33 f	65	55 m 52 f	107	56 m 67 f	123
Makaoliej	48 m 60 f	108	93 m 89 f	182	103 m 111 f	214
Rinamu	14 m 12 f	26	22 m 36 f	58	27 m 39 f	66
Subtotal	94 m 105 f	199	170 m 177 f	347	186 m 217 f	403
Other clans	9 m 10 f	19	52 m 60 f	112	65 m 72 f	137
Total	103 m 115 f	218	222 m 237 f	459	251 m 289 f	540

ior rank (M 3/3) had only four. For reasons which will become apparent, these two branches of Makaoliej were combined as one corporate lineage.

As indicated in Figure 3, most of the expansion of the small Rinamu sub-clan had occurred in the senior lineage (R 1) which had developed three segments (R 1/1, R 1/2, and R 1/3) with a total membership of twenty-five. The junior lineage (R 2) was in the process of becoming extinct as it had only one male.

Tables 3.2, 3.3, and 3.4 indicate the distribution of the Bikinians among the sub-clans. Table 3.2 reveals the clan affiliation of the 170 islanders who comprised the 1946 community; 164 of the 170 were members of the three sub-clans. The remaining six belonged to clans from other atolls. Four were spouses whom Bikinians had acquired from other communities and two were children (one was an adopted child; the other was the child of an inmarrying female). Three of the six were from the Rongelab community.

Table 3.3 indicates a total of thirty-five members of the Bikini sub-clans and thirteen islanders related to them were resident on other atolls. These were Bikini clansmen who had left

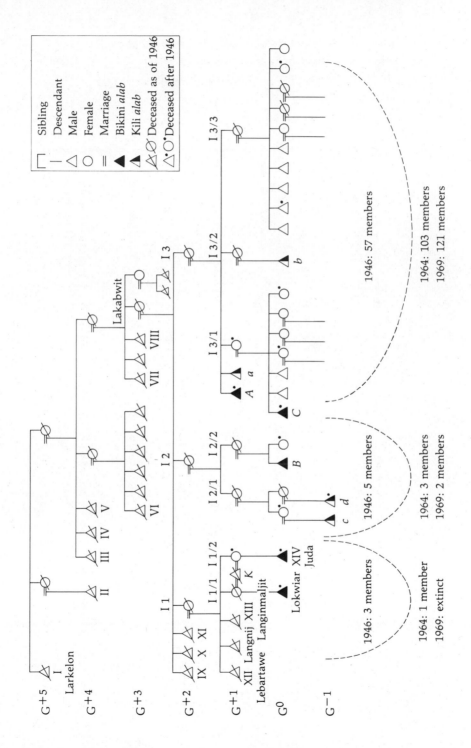

Figure 1. Ijjirik sub-clan.

the community in Japanese times, the spouses they had acquired from other communities, and all of their offspring. Approximately half of these were located on Ailinglablab Atoll where

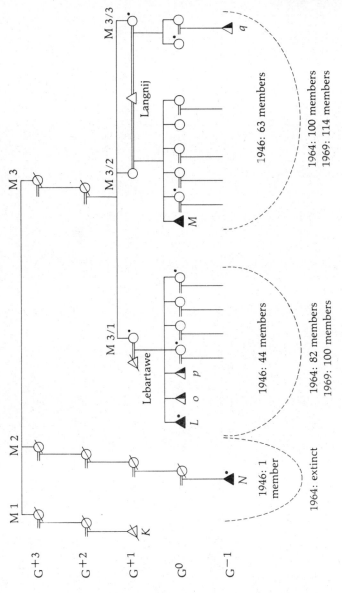

Figure 2. Makaoliej sub-clan.

the half-dozen Bikinians had once gone to serve in the household of the paramount chief. They had married into the local population, and after their period of servitude, they had decided to remain on Ailinglablab.

All other Bikinians who had left the community were living on four other atolls. Eight of them had remained in northern Ralik; four were married into the Rongelab community; and all four members of the Makaoliej lineage segment M 3/3 had been long-term residents of Lae Atoll where one of its females had formerly been married. One male had settled with a spouse on Ebon, the southernmost Ralik atoll. All other expatriates were members of two nuclear families located at Kwajalein.

With the exception of the Bikinians at Kwajalein and Rongelab, most of the islanders who had married and established residence elsewhere had not returned to the community, and their children had never set foot on Bikini's soil. Nonetheless, they were to become important to the community after its relocation. Table 3.4 is a compilation of Tables 3.2 and 3.3 and indicates the total number of Bikini clansmen and all of their non-Bikini relatives.

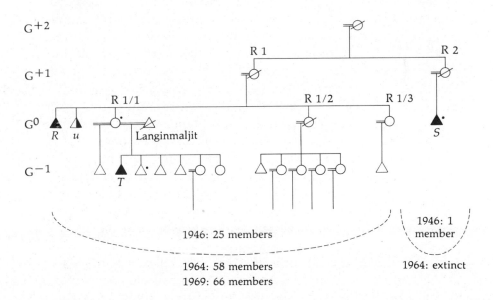

Figure 3. Rinamu sub-clan.

Kinship, Marriage, and Adoption

Kinship and Marriage. Because of clan exogamy and the endogamous character of the community imposed by Bikini's isolation, almost every Bikinian could trace one or more genealogical connections between himself and each of his fellow islanders. Bikinians thought of one another as *nukō* (a general term denoting 'my relative' or 'my kinsman'), and the idiom of kinship was extended to embrace the entire community.

The matrilineal organization, the principles by which individuals were ranked, and a preferential rule of bilateral cross-cousin marriage were reflected in kinship terminology and behavior. Perhaps because the relations among kin were so obvious in the small inbred community, terminology did not play an active role in identifying kinsmen. With the exception of real parents, a Bikinian invariably called relatives by personal names, and kin terms were used infrequently and primarily in referential contexts (see Table 3.5).

A Bikinian distinguished between kinsmen of the G^{+2} generation on the basis of sex. All females were *jibō* 'my grandmother', and all males were *jimmau* 'my grandfather'. In the G^{+1} generation, all females were *jinō* 'my mother'. Denoting the importance of the maternal uncle in the matrilineal system, all males of the G^{+1} generation within ego's sub-clan were designated by a common term *rikora* 'my mother's brother'; all other G^{+1} males were *jema* 'my father'. Within ego's own generation, real and classificatory parallel cousins of both sexes, real and classificatory cross-cousins of the same sex, and half-siblings were classed with full siblings. Reflecting the principle of relative chronological age, siblings were referred to as *jeō* 'my elder sibling' or *jatō* 'my younger sibling'. Potential marriage partners, that is, real and classificatory cross-cousins of the opposite sex, were identified by a special term, *rilikō*. The classification of kinsmen of the G^{-1} generation differed with the sex of the speaker. Female ego classed all G^{-1} kinsmen as *nejō* 'my child'. As a further demarcation of the mother's brother/sister's child relationship, male ego designated the children of his real and classificatory sisters within his sub-clan by the term *mangōrō* 'my sister's child', and classed all others as 'my child'. No distinctions were made among kin of

Table 3.5. Kinship Terminology (Third Person Singular, Male Speaker)

Term	Gloss
jibō	'grandmother' (all females of the second ascending generation)
jimmau	'grandfather' (all males of the second ascending generation)
jinō	'mother' (all females of the first ascending generation)
rikora	'mother's brother' (males of the first ascending generation who are members of speaker's sub-clan)
jema	'father' (males of the first ascending generation who are not members of speaker's sub-clan)
rilikō	'cross-cousin' (real and classificatory cross-cousins)
jeō	'older sibling' (full siblings, half-siblings, and real and classificatory parallel cousins older than speaker)
jatō	'younger sibling' (full siblings, half-siblings, and real and classificatory parallel cousins younger than speaker)
nejō	'child' (members of first descending generation who are not members of speaker's sub-clan)
mangōrō	'sister's child' (members of first descending generation who are members of speaker's sub-clan)
jibō	'grandchild' (all members of the second descending generation)

the G^{-2} generation; all were designated by the same term which denoted females of the G^{+2} generation regardless of their sex or the sex of the speaker.

Ideal norms of behavior were fairly consistent with terminological distinctions. Kinsmen were divided into two categories.

On the one hand, there were those with whom sexual relations
and marriage were theoretically *mo* 'forbidden' or *jekar* 'improper'. Comprising this category were siblings, kin of adjacent generations, and kin of alternate generations when they were members of the same sub-clan. Relations among siblings were formal
and restrained, and elder siblings received deference from younger
ones. The greatest restraint was among siblings of the opposite
sex; brothers and sisters avoided reference to the functions of the
body and were not together except in the company of others.
The restraint observed among real siblings, however, masked the
solidarity of the bond which united them. Real siblings thought
of themselves as a *bwij* founded by their mother, and they referred to themselves metaphorically as *einwōt juon* 'one in the
same' because they were from the same womb.

Parent/child relations were relatively informal, but parents
and children of the opposite sex treated each other with some
reserve and avoided jocularity with reference to sex and the body.
Relations between mother's brother/sister's child were quite formal, and the mother's brother was accorded great deference.[2]

Some inconsistency between terminological distinctions and
behavioral patterns was found among kin of alternate generations.
A privileged familiarity, including ribald jesting about sex, prevailed among all kinsmen of alternate generations. An incest pro-
hibition was coterminous with the rule of exogamy, however, and
it prohibited sexual relations between grandparent/grandchild of
the same sub-clan.

The second category of kinsmen consisted of those with
whom sex and marriage were appropriate. Sexual intercourse and
marriage between grandparent/grandchild not of the same sub-clan
were permissible and consistent with the joking relations between
the alternate generations. Such marital unions, however, were not
preferred or encouraged. Relations between cross-cousins of the
opposite sex were marked by extreme familiarity, and sexual rela-

---

[2] Considerable variation in the mother's brother/sister's child relationship
occurs in the Marshalls. At Majuro, the mother's brother is treated with
respect (Spoehr 1949:196-197), but the great deference found among Bikinians is apparently absent. On Arno Atoll, a joking relationship prevails between the mother's brother/sister's child (Rynkiewich 1972:51).

tions between them began in early adolescence. Marital unions between matrilateral (mother's brother's daughter) and patrilateral (father's sister's daughter) cross-cousins were equally appropriate and favored. Marriage with non-kin was also appropriate, but Bikini's isolation had always limited the availability of spouses from the outside.

In pre-mission times, polygyny was practiced. Sororal polygyny had been the most common form of plural union, but such marriages had always been few as only chiefs and the most prominent males had possessed the resources necessary to support more than a single spouse.

In most cases, marriages were contracted in a rather casual manner. After a period of pre-marital experimentation, individuals gradually settled into fairly stable unions with compatible partners. Marriage, however, was also a potential means of acquiring allies who could be called upon for support in intra-community conflicts. Although I have no statements from informants which indicate that marriages were specifically arranged for political ends, genealogical evidence suggests that males of chiefly status did upon occasion secure wives who provided them with particularly valuable allies.

As Table 3.6 indicates, the vast majority of marriages in the 1946 community were between cross-cousins and ninety-six percent of all marriages (twenty-five of twenty-nine) were approved unions. The demographic structure of the community, however, always influenced marriage patterns, and not every Bikinian could find a mate of the appropriate sub-clan, age, and generational standing in the small population. Thus, a few islanders were always faced with the choice of remaining single or violating ideal norms. As reflected in Table 3.6, four of the twenty-nine marriages in the community were considered improper unions, and they were referred to as the results of *bwir in lemnak* 'error in thinking'.[3]

---

[3] It has been argued elsewhere that the rule of preferential cross-cousin marriage and the relatively high frequency of both preferred and improper marital unions in the Bikini community were a function of the population's small size and its endogamous character due to its isolation from other atolls. All Marshallese express some notion that marital unions with cross-

Table 3.6. Bikini Marital Unions

Kin Ties between Spouses	1946 Married Couples		1964 Married Couples		1969 Married Couples	
	Resident at Bikini	Resident elsewhere	Resident at Kili	Resident elsewhere	Resident at Kili	Resident elsewhere
Approved unions						
Real cross-cousins	6	3	8	4	9	3
Classificatory cross-cousins	14		21	1	24	1
Classificatory grandparent/ grandchild	1		1		2	
No kin tie [a]	4	9	8	24	11	29
Subtotal	25	12	38	29	46	33
Improper unions						
Classificatory parent/child	3		5		6	
Classificatory siblings	1		1		1	
Subtotal	4		6		7	
Total	29	12	44	29	53	33

[a] Marital union with a non-Bikinian.

Table 3.6 also indicates the number of marriages which had been contracted by the thirty-five members of the three sub-clans who were not part of the 1946 community. Three of the expatri-

---

cousins are desirable. In large populations, however, in which a great number of non-kin are available, most islanders marry non-kin and the incidence of both cross-cousin unions and improper matings is very low. In contrast and because of the numerous kin ties which linked all members of the small inbred Bikini community, all individuals of the same generation were related either as cross-cousins or siblings (classificatory parallel cousins), and individuals had no alternative but to marry a kinsman of an approved type (grandparents not of ego's sub-clan, as well as cross-cousins) or violate ideal norms (Kiste and Rynkiewich, forthcoming).

ates were married to fellow Bikinians; other unions were with islanders from other atolls.

Adoption. The practice of *kokajiriri* which may be roughly
glossed as 'adoption' was quite common. At least one-fourth of
the Bikinians had been adopted as children, but my data are incomplete, and the number of adoptions was much greater.

Adoptions were casually arranged and could be initiated by
any individual, married or unmarried. Usually, a request to adopt
was made to the parents of a newborn child. Theoretically, the
parents could refuse, but this was unlikely as the would-be adop-
ter(s) was almost always a close relative. Most commonly, siblings adopted one another's children, and grandparents frequently
adopted their grandchildren.

Adoption did not alienate a child from his biological parents;
instead, an adopted child acquired an additional set of parents
who looked after his welfare and contributed to his or her personal security. The relations between foster parents and adopted
child varied considerably in intensity and content however.[4] In
some instances, the relationship was no more than nominal; as a
youngster, the adopted child received attention from his foster
parents, but later in life, the bond was all but forgotten. In other
cases, the child alternated between the residences of his two sets
of parents or took up permanent residence with his foster parents,
and the bond endured throughout their lifetimes. Regardless of
the variations in the relationship, the practice of adoption functioned to reinforce the ties of kinship which already existed between relatives and family groups.

Politics and Land

The sub-clans, lineages, and the network of relations among
kinsmen were the structural frameworks which were important

---

[4] The distinction between 'fosterage' (temporarily taking care of other's
children as an obligation of kinship) and 'adoption' (permanently assuming
the major responsibilities of natural parents) that is made in many Oceania
societies cannot be made for the Marshalls. For a discussion of these concepts see Carroll 1970:3-17.

for determining succession to statuses of political authority and the inheritance of rights to land. Succession and inheritance were closely related processes, but they were structurally distinct and must be conceptually separated.

Each sub-clan, lineage, and lineage segment had a head known as *alab*. The heads of the three sub-clans were referred to as *luk-un alab* 'major headman'; the head of the Ijjirik sub-clan was the successor of the legendary Larkelon and was the traditional chief. He directed the everyday affairs of the community, mediated disputes, and bore the primary responsibility of managing the Bikinians' relations with outsiders. He was directly responsible to the paramount chief, and it was his duty to see that the community met its tribute obligation.

The heads of Makaoliej and Rinamu were subordinate to the Ijjirik chief, but each represented his own sub-clan when tribute was rendered to the paramount chief. With regard to the community's internal affairs, each was the principal spokesman for his fellow clansmen, and within the sub-clan his views and opinions carried far more influence than that of the lesser *alab*. The heads of the sub-clans received first fruit offerings from their fellow clansmen and, reflecting the authority structure of the community, the Makaoliej and Rinamu heads gave a portion of what they received to the Ijjirik chief. He in turn usually redistributed part of the offerings he received according to situational variables.

Theoretically, the head of any sub-clan, lineage, or lineage segment was its senior ranking male, and upon his death, others succeeded according to the principles of relative age and seniority of generation. Within the sub-clans which were composed of more than one lineage, and within lineages which consisted of more than one segment, however, the principles of relative age and seniority of generation sometimes proved in conflict. As cultural norms did not specify either principle as having priority over the other for determining rank and succession, there was a structural ambiguity in the system. For example, when the heads of the lineages of a sub-clan were of the same generation (that is, when the lineage heads were classificatory brothers), the head of the senior lineage was clearly of superior rank and was the uncontested head of the sub-clan. When the head of a senior lineage

was a member of a generation below that of the head of a junior
lineage (in such instances, the head of the senior lineage was usually the classificatory maternal nephew of the head of the junior
lineage), the principles did not specify either as being superior in
rank, and there were no rules determining succession. Such structural ambiguity led to disputes between members of a sub-clan.
Actual succession was determined by the maneuvers of separate
interest groups and the support they could muster within the
framework of the sub-clan, and in some instances, from the other
two sub-clans.

Similarly, uncertainty sometimes occurred over the succession to the headship of a lineage that was composed of a number
of segments with a depth of two or more generations. Such uncertainties were often resolved by any one of several situational
variables. For example, when the head of a senior segment was
both young (immature adolescent or child) and a member of a
generation lower than the head of a junior segment, the latter
was recognized as the lineage head. Also, males who were im-
paired by age or other infirmities were usually bypassed as can-
didates for lineage head. In some instances, however, when males
of senior and junior segments competed for the right to succeed
to the headship of a lineage, fission occurred and, as a result of
conflict or consensus, a lineage would divide into separate corporate lineages.

The System of Land Rights. Except in lineages that were
becoming extinct, the typical corporate lineage had a depth of
three or four generations. As a lineage expanded in size and
depth over time, its holdings became divided among its segments
which in turn emerged as corporate lineages in their own right.
As noted above, the fission of a lineage often occurred as a result of conflict or consensus among lineage mates. The typical
land parcel of a lineage's estate was a strip of land known as a
wāto that traversed the width of an island from lagoon beach to
ocean reef. In all cases, a lineage's estate was composed of a
number of such parcels on several islands in the atoll.

An important distinction was made between two kinds of
alab; those who controlled land and those who did not. The
head of a corporate lineage was both *alab in bwij* 'head of line-

age' and *alab in brij* 'head of land'. A male inherited the *alab* rights to his lineage's land at the same time he succeeded to the headship of the lineage. A male who headed a segment of a lineage that was only part of a larger corporate lineage was also known as *alab in bwij* (in this instance, head of a lineage segment). He was treated with respect by the members of his lineage segment and had some influence among them, but he possessed no real power or authority. A male who had acquired land from sources outside his lineage was 'head of land', but he was not necessarily 'head of lineage'.[5]

The duties and privileges of the head of a corporate lineage distinguished him from his lineage mates. He had authority over the use of the lineage's land and oversaw the distribution of its resources. The headman had always been entitled to a disproportionate share of resources from the land, and with the introduction of the copra trade, he gained additional advantage and power over his lineage mates when the same practice was extended to income derived from the cash crop. The lineage head retained one-fourth of the cash; some he used for personal wants, and theoretically, he kept a reserve fund which he controlled and allocated among his lineage mates when they were in need. The headman also represented the interests of his lineage in community affairs. Lineage members under his authority were *rijerbal ro* 'workers'. They had inalienable rights to their lineage's land; those rights may be referred to as 'worker rights' which entitled the lineage member to a share of the land's resources and the privilege of residing upon it.

---

[5] Other Marshallese do not make an explicit distinction between *alab in brij* and *alab in bwij*. An example of how a male could hold the former status and not the latter is provided in Figure 3 with *alab T. T*'s elder half-brother was the offspring of their mother's first marriage; *T* and his five younger siblings were fathered by their mother's second husband. As children belonged to the lineage of their mother regardless of their paternity, the entire sibling set belonged to her lineage, and they formed the segment R 1/1 of the larger corporate lineage R 1 headed by their mother's brother, *alab R.* The segment R 1/1 was headed by *T*'s elder half-brother as he was the eldest of the sibling set and was thus 'head of lineage (segment)'. *T*, however, was 'head of land' which he and his younger siblings had received from their father.

The spouses of lineage members and the children of lineage males had use rights to the lineage's land, and they also shared in its products and could reside upon it. Children often grew up on a portion of their father's lineage land. Later, as married adults, they could and often did continue to exercise their usufruct. Individuals not belonging to the lineage but who had been adopted by its members were sometimes given usufruct rights to a portion of the estate. Adoption did not necessarily entail the provision of such rights which were given only when the bond between the adopter and adopted were particularly close.

The rights of individuals outside the lineage were not inalienable. A spouse's usufruct was always terminated with divorce and usually ended with the death of his or her mate. The usufruct rights of children of lineage males could be terminated by members of their father's lineage after his death unless other provisions were made. The specific rights granted to individuals adopted from outside the lineage varied greatly; in some instances,

Plate 5. Two Bikini headmen and youth perched on the boom of an outrigger canoe, 1946. *(Photo by Carl Mydans. Time-Life, Inc.)*

the adopted individual was given only occasional use rights. In other cases, usufruct rights similar to those of the children of lineage males were granted.

The estate of a lineage was clearly distinguished from two other categories of property: (1) land to which a set of siblings had received both *alab* and worker rights from their father, and (2) gift land or land to which an individual had received rights in exchange for a service rendered. Only an *alab* who was both 'head of lineage' and 'head of land' could dispose of his lineage's land in either of these two ways. In the event that an *alab* was the sole surviving member of his lineage, his children gained the equivalent of lineage worker rights to their father's land, and upon his death, they inherited all rights to it. If, however, an *alab* were the head of a viable lineage, he supposedly obtained the consent of his lineage mates before he could set aside land for himself and his children. In either case, a male and his children who held land together comprised a patri-centered corporation.

The eldest male of a set of siblings who formed a corporation with their father became the *alab* with authority over the land upon the latter's death. His rights as *alab* were equal to those of the heads of the corporate lineages, and he represented the interests of his siblings in community affairs. The siblings had three alternatives as to how they could manage the land. One option was to hold the land as a matrilineage composed only of themselves and their matrilineal offspring (the children of the female members of the sibling set). Secondly, the land could be given to the children of the males who had first acquired it from their father, that is, once land had been alienated from a lineage, *alab* and worker rights could be inherited through males. Lastly, siblings could and commonly did employ a combination of the first two options. In any case, land that siblings received from their father was theirs and theirs alone. Neither the head of their own lineage nor other lineage mates had claim to it. When it was clearly agreed that an *alab* had secured for his children *alab* and worker rights to a portion of his lineage's land, subsequent headmen of his lineage had no authority or claim (including usufruct) upon it.

The particulars in any given case, however, were not always

clearly defined. The alternative forms of inheritance provided
both a certain flexibility in the land tenure system and a set of
mechanisms which were manipulated as islanders attempted to
maximize the amount of land to which they could claim some
right. Children who had been exercising their usufruct to a parcel
of their father's lineage land sometimes attempted to continue doing so after his death and claimed that they had received *alab* and
worker rights to it. Those claims were rejected by the members
of their father's lineage, but such disputes were seldom permanently resolved. Discussions of Bikini land rights were still the source
of heated arguments over two decades after relocation, and if the
behavior of Bikinians observed on Kili provides any indication of
the past, each party involved in a land dispute sometimes exploited the land parcel under litigation while protesting the other's
claim to it.

Gift land given in exchange for a service rendered was not
common. In one known instance, chiefs rewarded an ally who
had supported them in intra-community conflicts with land. This
transaction occurred at about the turn of the century, and in the
decades prior to relocation, only one land parcel was given in payment for a service. The recipient constructed a canoe for an *alab,*
and he received all rights to a land parcel with full authority over
its disposition.

The Struggle for Land and Power. The ways in which Bikinians competed for land and the actual patterns of inheritance
had changed since the turn of the century as they had responded
to the peace imposed by Europeans and as they had attempted to
cope with the disparities which had developed among the sizes of
the respective lineages. Thus, the very recent history of Bikini
land tenure can only be understood against the background of
earlier times.

In the pre-European era, through German times and most of
the Japanese period, the senior Ijjirik lineage held a vastly disproportionate amount of land. Its holdings constituted a warrant for
the chiefly status of its head. As evidenced by the history of the
succession of the Bikini chiefs, competition over the office of
chief and control of the chiefly lands was the source of perpetual
conflict. Ideal relations among kinsmen were ignored, and Ijjirik

males engaged in a power struggle which witnessed few lulls; in at least two instances, a Makaoliej *alab* was involved in the conflicts.

According to the reported genealogy, the legendary Larkelon was succeeded by his maternal nephews, chiefs II through V of the dynasty. Nothing is remembered of the circumstances of their succession. As Figure 1 indicates, Larkelon's nephews had two sisters who founded the senior and junior Ijjirik lineages, and they were succeeded by their eldest sister's eldest son, chief VI. He had five younger brothers within the senior lineage. None, however, lived to succeed him. All were assassinated by ambitious males of the junior lineage, and its eldest male came to power as chief VII.

Chief VII had two younger brothers and two sisters, the eldest of whom was Lakabwit whose daughters founded the lineages which comprised the Ijjirik sub-clan in the decades prior to relocation. Chief VII and one of his brothers were murdered in an abortive coup by their youngest sister's two sons. After the latter's failure to seize the chieftainship, VII's surviving brother succeeded to office as chief VIII. The fate of the youngest sister's sons is not remembered, but they left no descendants, and it is probable that they were eliminated after their unsuccessful rebellion. These events occurred during the time of the G^{+3} and G^{+2} Ijjirik generations, and as a consequence, the sub-clan was reduced to a single lineage composed of chief VIII, his sister Lakabwit, her three sons and three daughters, and the offspring of the latter. Chief VIII was the victim of another assassination, the details of which are not entirely clear. He was succeeded by Lakabwit's eldest son, chief IX. It appears that some degree of harmony prevailed for a time as the string of assassinations was broken; chief IX died of natural causes and was peacefully succeeded by his next younger brother, chief X.

Chief X and his younger brother were of the G^{+2} generation. During his reign, his eldest sister's three sons formed a particularly powerful alliance through the marriage of their sisters to *alab K*, the head of the Makaoliej sub-clan (*K* was the head of the then senior Makaoliej lineage M 1). As Figure 1 indicates, the eldest of chief X's maternal nephews was a certain Lebartawe, the second was Langnij, the youngest was Langinmaljit, and the brothers had two sisters. The head of the Makaoliej sub-clan was married to both of the latter, and he was the father of Lebartawe's only two maternal nephews and potential successors, Lokwiar and Juda, the last males of the senior Ijjirik lineage. The Makaoliej *alab* assassinated chief X, and later, he joined forces with Lebartawe, his two brothers, and his own son Lokwiar when they eliminated chief X's brother who had been chief XI for a brief time.[6]

Lebartawe was the last of the Bikini chiefs to come to power by the murder of his predecessor and rival. He succeeded to office not long before the German administration extended its influence into the northern atolls and the mission was established at Bikini in 1908. Armed conflicts within the community were brought to an end just as they had been curtailed at an earlier date in most of the southern Marshalls.

This brief history of the succession of Bikini chiefs reveals that no less than ten males were killed in the hostilities endemic in Ijjirik. Men conspired against their maternal uncles, and the senior lineage was always under the potential threat of junior lines as Ijjirik males fought over the prizes of chiefly status and land. The motives of *alab K* seem equally clear; he advanced the position of his own two sons, Lokwiar and Juda, within the chiefly lineage, and he was awarded land by Lebartawe and his brothers.[7]

Given the enforced peace, Lebartawe lived to quite an advanced age, and he remained chief throughout most of the Japanese period. The islanders remember him as the last of the Ij-

---

[6] It would seem unlikely that conflicts over the chieftainship prior to Lebartawe's time were limited to Ijjirik males, but I have no evidence which specifically indicates the involvement of others in earlier assassinations.

[7] Bikinians today claim that Lebartawe and his brothers gave land to the Makaoliej *alab* for the sole reason that they were brothers-in-law, and that the gifts had nothing to do with the assassinations. On sociological grounds this explanation seems rather implausible. Comtemporary informants are explicit as to what was at stake in the feuds among Ijjirik males, however. President John F. Kennedy was assassinated during the period of my first fieldwork among the Bikinians. The latter immediately assumed that Lee Harvey Oswald would succeed to the Presidency, and the islanders were never satisfied with my explanations as to why he could not. To them, the event made no sense if the assassin or his patron could not succeed his victim and fall heir to his property.

jirik chiefs to have "really ruled" Bikini for he was the last of
the chiefs to have controlled a great amount of land.

The chiefs had always utilized their landholdings to gain
supporters within the community. Some land had been alienated
from the chiefly lineage by Lebartawe's predecessors two generations earlier when they had acquired the two Rinamu females as
spouses from Rongelab. As their Rinamu offspring were landless
on Bikini, the chiefs had provided them with land which became
Rinamu lineage property. These land grants secured for the
chiefs the allegiance of their Rinamu children but did not substantially reduce the holdings of the chiefly lineage; the senior
Ijjirik males still controlled a major portion of Bikini when Lebartawe came to power.

Additional land was alienated from the chiefly lineage early
in Lebartawe's reign when he and his brothers gave land to their
Makaoliej ally, *alab K.* This did not, however, represent a permanent loss of land from the chiefly lineage because *alab K* was
the last survivor of his own lineage (M 1) and the land he controlled would thus be inherited by his own two sons, Lokwiar
and Juda, of the chiefly lineage. During Lebartawe's reign, however, other circumstances resulted in the wholesale alienation of
land from the control of the chiefs; those circumstances were
directly related to the growing disparities among the memberships
of the sub-clans and lineages. Most of these have already been
described, but their most salient features and certain important
facts which have not been made explicit may be summarized as
follows:

1. The disparity among Ijjirik lineages occurred during Lebartawe's reign. The third and junior most lineage (I 3) was in the
process of expansion. This occurred just at the time that the two
senior ranking lineages were declining in size and that Lebartawe
and his brothers had only Lokwiar and Juda as potential heirs and
successors within their own lineage.

2. Lokwiar and Juda were not only in a favored position
within the senior Ijjirik lineage; they were also the heirs apparent
of their own father, *alab K,* head of Makaoliej, for reasons which
have been indicated above.

3. As indicated in Figures 2 and 3, Lebartawe and his two

brothers were the progenitors of all the expanding lineages of
Makaoliej and one segment of Rinamu. More specifically:

a. Lebartawe and his next eldest brother, Langnij, were
the spouses of the three G^{+1} generation females of the junior Makaoliej line (M 3) and had fathered all of their numerous children. (In 1946, 105 of the 108 members of Makaoliej were the progeny of Lebartawe, Langnij, and the three
G^{+1} Makaoliej females.)

b. Langinmaljit, the youngest of Lebartawe's brothers,
was the spouse of the eldest female of the senior Rinamu
lineage (the founder of lineage segment R 1/1), and he was
the progenitor of her six youngest children and four grandchildren. (These ten comprised about forty percent of all
Rinamu sub-clan in 1946.)

During the years of Lebartawe's reign, the concentration of
land in the chiefly lineage and the growing demographic imbal-
ance among the sub-clans and their constituent lineages required
that some redistribution of land occur to meet the needs of those
rapidly expanding lineages.[8] The response of Lebartawe and his
two brothers was relatively simple—they allocated some of their
holdings to the second and third ranking Ijjirik lineages. As the
number of their own Makaoliej and Rinamu children increased,
Lebartawe and his brothers gave them land belonging to the senior Ijjirik lineage and specified that they were to receive both
alab and worker rights to it.

As a consequence of this redistribution of land by chiefly
males, the siblings of the G^0 generation of Makaoliej lineage
M 3/1 formed one corporation which held the land received
from their father Lebartawe as well as that which they had inherited matrilineally. The half-siblings of the Makaoliej lines

---

[8] Maintaining an equitable distribution of land among matrilineal descent
groups is a reoccurring problem in many Micronesian societies because of
the great fluctuation in the size of the membership of the groups within
short time spans; the problem has been discussed by Goodenough (1955),
and Rynkiewich (1972) has provided an extended case study of the problem
on Arno Atoll in the southern Marshalls. In the Bikini case, problems arising
from inequities in the landholdings of the several lineages were compounded
by the concentration of land in the chiefly lineage.

M 3/2 and M 3/3 combined to form another corporation which held the land received from their father Langnij and that which they inherited matrilineally. Langinmaljit's children within the senior Rinamu lineage segment R 1/1 became a separate corporation within their own lineage, and Langinmaljit's eldest son (male T in Figure 3, see Footnote 5) became an *alab* with authority over land.

As Lebartawe and his brothers alienated more and more of their chiefly land, they created steadfast allies among their numerous Makaoliej and Rinamu children, but by the time of the demise of the youngest of the brothers, the power and influence traditionally associated with the chieftainship were greatly diminished because of the drastic reduction in their holdings. Lokwiar and Juda inherited what remained of the chiefly land. They were somewhat compensated for the reduced chiefly holdings, however, when upon the death of their father, *alab K*, they inherited all rights to the land of the senior Makaoliej lineage M 1.

The redistribution of the senior Ijjirik lineage's land had far reaching consequences for the entire community. The prevailing pattern of matrilineal inheritance of land rights was altered for an entire generation of Bikinians. In 1946, approximately fifty-eight percent of all land parcels in the atoll had passed from males to their own children and most of this situation was accounted for by the transfer of land from the senior Ijjirik lineage to the children of the three chiefly males and by Lokwiar and Juda's inheritance of their own father's land (Kiste 1968:190-201).

More importantly, the numerous father-to-child transfers of land rights resulted in a realignment of power within the community. The Makaoliej lineages M 3/1 and M 3/2−M 3/3 became the major landholding corporations, and their heads and members gained substantial power and influence. Further, the power and influence of the two lineages plus the weight of their numerical strength also appear to have been instrumental in determining succession to the headship of the Makaoliej sub-clan. With the death of Lokwiar and Juda's father, the senior Makaoliej lineage M 1 became extinct, and lineage M 2 became senior in rank. As indicated, M 2 had never had more than a few members, and by 1946, it had been reduced to a single survivor, *alab N*. As Figure 2 indicates, *alab N* was of the G^{-1} generation while *alab L* of the next ranking lineage M 3/1 was of the higher G^0 generation; hence, the principles governing rank and succession did not specify which of the two was the ranking *alab* of the sub-clan and was entitled to succeed to its headship. Despite such structural ambiguity, there is no evidence to suggest that the outcome was ever in doubt. The faction favoring the succession of *alab L* was overwhelming; he had the support of his own large lineage, and he had the prestige of being Lebartawe's son. *Alab N* could never have offered a serious challenge to *L*'s succession, and the latter was recognized as the head of Makaoliej without contest.

The chiefly land acquired by Rinamu *alab T* and his younger siblings also altered the relative spheres of power and influence among Rinamu clansmen. *Alab T* and his younger siblings enjoyed a particularly favorable position; they continued to possess rights to the land of their own Rinamu lineage R 1 under the authority of their mother's brother, *alab R,* head of the Rinamu sub-clan. As the land they had acquired from their father was free from the authority of their mother's brother, they had an autonomy of their own, and *alab T* emerged as an influential headman in his own right.

With the probable exception of *alab N,* Makaoliej clansmen were quite satisfied with the redistribution of land and power as were the Rinamu *alab T* and his younger siblings. There were others, however, who were discontent with the manner in which the chiefs had disposed of their land, and they were of the firm conviction that the children of the chiefly males had acquired an inequitable amount. The greatest unrest was among males of the junior Ijjirik lineage I 3. The head of the lineage, *alab A,* and his younger brother, male *a* in Figure 1, were members of Lebartawe's G^{+1} generation, and they had ambitions to succeed to the chieftainship and acquire control of the land the chiefs had alienated from Ijjirik. The younger brother was the most vociferous and aggressive in advancing the cause of the junior lineage. He and some of his lineage mates claimed that the chiefly holdings should never have passed from Ijjirik hands, and further, they charged that when Lebartawe redistributed land their lineage had been deprived of an equitable share. *Alab A* and his brother were strongly supported by their eldest sister's eldest son; he was an *alab* with authority over land in his own right (*alab C* in Figure 1) be-

ing the sole recipient of gift land in the years immediately prior
to relocation.

The discontent of the junior Ijjirik males came to a head
around the time of the American occupation of the islands. Lebartawe, having outlived his next eldest brother, had died shortly
before the Americans' arrival. Langinmaljit, the youngest brother,
was quite aged when he succeeded as chief, and he died soon
after. Upon his death, the absence of structural priorities among
the rules governing rank and succession provided the males of
the junior Ijjirik lineage with the opportunity to advance their
own interests and attempt to secure the chieftainship for their
own *alab A*. They argued that he was of the same generation as
Lebartawe and his brothers and was thus entitled to succeed them
as chief. Lokwiar and Juda countered their claim by contending
that males of a senior lineage always succeeded before males of
junior ranking lineages (the example of the succession of *alab L*
to the headship of Makaoliej sub-clan notwithstanding). The head
of the second ranking Ijjirik lineage I 2, *alab B,* supported Lokwiar and Juda. As later events would prove, he was an ambitious
man, and his reasons for casting his lot with the senior lineage
males were obvious. He was a member of their generation and it
was thus to his advantage to have males of a senior ranking lineage succeed to the chieftainship before those of a junior lineage.

Few other details pertaining to the dispute are known. Both
Ijjirik factions could claim some support from affinal relatives in
the powerful Makaoliej lineages, but it is almost certain that the
Makaoliej clansmen favored Lokwiar and Juda because the males
of the junior Ijjirik lineage had opposed the transfer of chiefly
land to Makaoliej. It is known that the majority of the *alab* eventually recognized Lokwiar and Juda as the legitimate successors
to their mothers' brothers. However, the long reign of Lebartawe
had the important consequence for Lokwiar that he, like Langinmaljit before him, was quite aged and infirm when he finally
came to office, and he voluntarily relinquished the chieftainship
to Juda who was in his mid-forties. By prior agreement, they divided the land they had inherited, and both enjoyed the status
of *alab* with authority over land. Juda succeeded as chief, and
as previously noted, he was named to the position of magistrate
when that office and the institution of the council were introduced by the Americans.

The issue was not resolved, however, to the satisfaction of the junior Ijjirik males. They charged that Juda had acquired the chieftainship because he had presented himself as chief of the community to the Americans when they arrived at Bikini and that because of their ignorance or disregard of Marshallese traditions they had accepted him at face value. An undercurrent of discontent remained focused within the junior Ijjirik lineage, and as a result of their protestations, military government officials had the matter investigated when the first anthropological study of the community was conducted at Rongerik. Informants supported Juda ". . . as the rightful heir to the position without question" (Mason 1948:12).

The thwarted ambitions of the males of the junior Ijjirik lineage were similar to those which had precipitated the assassinations and violent conflicts of earlier times. Unlike the pre-colonial era, however, the males of junior rank had no effective means of achieving their aspirations. Even though the traditional power of the chief had largely been eroded due to the alienation of once-chiefly land, the dispute over the succession of Juda was clear evidence that the office was still a valued political prize. While there is no evidence to support the contention that Juda acquired the chieftainship by gaining the support of the Americans, there is no doubt that his status as head of the community was enhanced when he was named magistrate and was recognized as such by the adminstration. Accusations of the males of the junior Ijjirik lineage were an early indication and accurate recognition of the fact that nontraditional means of securing power and influence had indeed been introduced. Subsequent events show that Juda took full advantage of American support and recognition to further establish his own base of authority at the head of the community.

Regardless of differences of opinion pertaining to succession to the chieftainship and the inheritance of land rights, the eleven men who were the traditional leaders of the community in 1946 were those who had emerged as *alab in brij* 'head of land' because of land transfers in the decades prior to relocation. Hereafter, these men may simply be referred to as the eleven Bikini *alab*. As may be observed in Figures 1, 2, and 3, the eleven were not of equal rank within the structure of the lineages of the sub-clans, but nonetheless, having authority over land, they possessed power

and influence over their fellows. They were the males who directed the affairs of the community and who had formed the
council at the suggestion of the Americans.

Five of the *alab* were of Ijjirik sub-clan, three were Makaoliej, and three were Rinamu. As reflected in Figures 1, 2, and 3
and in some of the foregoing discussion, four of the eleven *alab*
(Lokwiar, Juda, *alab N,* and *alab S*) headed patri-centered landholding corporations because they were the last surviving members of their lineages. *Alab B* of the second ranking Ijjirik lineage headed both a patri-centered corporation and a corporate
lineage. Employing the father-to-child alternative to matrilineal
inheritance, he had established his own children on land which
he had inherited *alab* rights from his father, and he had specified
that his sons would succeed him on that land. Land inherited
matrilineally was held with his lineage mates, and his maternal
nephews were his heirs apparent on it.[9] *Alab C* of the Ijjirik
lineage segment I 3/1 was unique in that he held his parcel of
gift land as an individual. *Alab T* within the Rinamu lineage segment R 1/1 headed the corporation composed of himself and his
younger siblings, and it was not yet discernible as to how they
would manage the future disposition of the estate which had recently been received from their father. The remaining four *alab*
were heads of corporate lineages. Table 3.7 provides a summary
list of the Bikini *alab,* their position in the structure of the sub-
clans, and the type of corporations they headed.

The Council. The council form of government with the position of magistrate not only enhanced chief Juda's status as head
of the community but also provided all of the *alab* with official
recognition as men of authority and responsibility within the administrative system created by the Americans. At the suggestion
of the Americans, the council met once each month, and the deliberations of the traditional leaders were conducted with a greater degree of formality than in earlier times.

---

[9] *Alab B* was head of the second ranking lineage in Ijjirik even though he belonged to its junior ranking segment (see Figure 1). At the time he succeeded to office, both of his maternal (classificatory) nephews in the senior segment were youths and could not have offered any serious opposition to his
succession.

Table 3.7. The Eleven Bikini *Alab,* 1946

Alab	Sub-clan	Lineage or lineage segment	Type of corporation headed by the *alab*
Lokwiar	Ijjirik	I 1	Patri-centered
Juda	Ijjirik	I 1	Patri-centered
Alab B	Ijjirik	I 2	Patri-centered and matrilineage
Alab A	Ijjirik	I 3	Matrilineage
Alab C	Ijjirik	I 3/1	Gift land held as an individual
Alab N	Makaoliej	M 2	Patri-centered
Alab L	Makaoliej	M 3/1	Matrilineage
Alab M	Makaoliej	M 3/2—3/3	Matrilineage
Alab R	Rinamu	R 1	Matrilineage
Alab S	Rinamu	R 2	Patri-centered
Alab T	Rinamu	R 1/1	Land held with younger siblings

The council contained three officers in addition to the magistrate. According to the American plan, the officer second in authority to the magistrate was the scribe, *rijeje* 'one who writes'; he was charged with the responsibility of maintaining census records and recording council decisions. The other two officials were policemen, *rikalwijirak* 'one who stops'. The council officers received small salaries paid by the administration, and thus the incumbents held nontraditional positions of some influence and economic advantage in the community.[10]

With the exception of Juda's selection as magistrate, males named to occupy the council offices only partially reflected the traditional authority structure of the community. First, the aged Lokwiar was usually represented in council by his eldest son who

---

[10] At a later date, each community in the Marshalls was made responsible for the payment of its council officers. Most communities meet this obligation by levying a head tax on their members.

would succeed him as *alab*. Apparently because he possessed the requisite skills, Lokwiar's son was selected as the scribe, and he was thus second in authority to Juda within the formal structure of the council. Secondly, of the two policemen, one was a man of little importance, and the other was *alab B,* head of the second ranking Ijjirik lineage. Within the council, *alab B* was subordinate to the scribe, but in reality, his rank within Ijjirik gave him a much more influential role. When Juda succeeded to the chieftainship, it was generally assumed that *alab B* was next in the line of succession, and he came to occupy the role of Juda's confidant and executive officer. While not hesitant to voice his own opinions, he generally supported Juda in community affairs and saw that his directions were carried out.

Residence and Community

Households. Rights to land determined the location and residential choices of the eleven *alab,* and their influence was reflected in the domestic organization of the community. The islanders were divided among eleven family groups or households, each headed by an *alab.* There was no indigenous term denoting this social unit, but the Bikinians sometimes referred to it as *bamli* 'family', a word they had learned from missionaries.

The households were situated on the lagoon beach and were widely dispersed over adjacent land parcels in the central portion of Bikini Island (see Map 5). The members of a household shared two or three dwellings and a cookhouse. The dwellings were twenty-six in number and were primarily used as sleeping quarters and shelter from inclement weather since most activities were carried on outdoors. The focal point of each household was the cookhouse; household members contributed to a common larder, prepared food together, and accomplished tasks associated with everyday life.

The households of nine of the *alab* were located on land over which they had authority. Eight of the nine had acquired their residential sites from their fathers and had succeeded the latter as household heads. The residence of the other *alab* was located on matrilineally inherited land; this was the sole instance

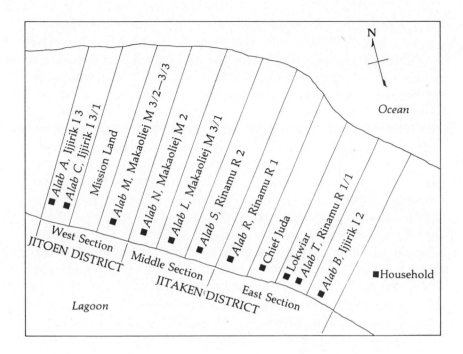

Map 5.   Reconstruction of household sites on Bikini.

of a male who had succeeded his mother's brother as both *alab*
and household head. Of the remaining two *alab*, neither had
land on the main island, and they had to reside on the land of
another *alab*. One was the Rinamu *alab T*, the son of Lebartawe's
youngest brother, Langinmaljit. The latter's household had been
located on land held by the senior Ijjirik lineage which had been
inherited by Lokwiar. When *alab T* had succeeded his father as
head of the domestic unit, Lokwiar had allowed him to remain
on the land. The other *alab* without land on the main island was
alab C of Ijjirik lineage segment I 3/1 who held the only parcel
of gift land; he had established a household adjacent to that of
his mother's brother, *alab A*, on land which was under the latter's authority.

    The households were quite flexible units, with considerable
variation in size and composition. They ranged in size from
twenty-five to seven members with an average of about fifteen.
As one reflection of the system of land rights, the households

were largely cognatic in structure.[11] In the early years of marriage, young Bikinians had a tendency to reside with the female's household more often than with the male's, but there was no preferred rule of residence. As individuals had rights to both their fathers' and their spouses' land as well as rights to the estate of their own lineage, a married couple could affiliate with either the husband's or the wife's parental households. The households were in a constant state of flux as shifts in residence easily occurred, and some young marrieds moved occasionally between parental households. Young children moved freely between the residences of real, classificatory, and foster parents. The composition of the households as they existed immediately prior to relocation is presented as Tables 3.8 and 3.9. It must be emphasized that the data in the tables do not reflect the flexibility of the households and necessarily present only a static picture of their composition at a certain point in time.[12]

The variation in the size and composition of households reflected both their flexibility and the differential stages of a general developmental cycle. As indicated in Table 3.8, four of the households (those headed by Juda, Lokwiar, *alab N,* and *alab S*) were cognatic extended families composed of some of the heads' unmarried children, and some of their married children with their own spouses and offspring. Five others had once been similar to the above four, but they had been transformed into or were in the process of becoming joint sibling families; see Table 3.9. In each case, the former household head was deceased and had been succeeded by his eldest son (or in one case, his sister's son), and the composition of each was determined by the sex and number of married and unmarried siblings who continued to

---

[11] Cognatic refers to the tracing of kinship relations through either males or females. The core of each Bikini cognatic extended family was comprised of an older couple and some of their married and unmarried children of either sex. Affinal relatives were also included.

[12] The abbreviations used here and in subsequent tables have the following meanings: mo = mother; fa = father; si = sister; br = brother; da = daughter; so = son; ch = child; wi = wife; hu = husband; gr = grand. Combinations of abbreviations are to be read as follows: da hu = daughter's husband; si da hu br = sister's daughter's husband's brother.

Table 3.8. Cognatic Extended Families

Alab at Head of Household	Juda	Lokwiar	*Alab N* Makaoliej M 2	*Alab S* Rinamu R 2
Alab	1	1	1	1
Alab's mo	1			
Alab's wi	1	1	1	1
Alab's so	2	1	5	2
Alab's so wi		1	1	2
Alab's da	4	5	3	3
Alab's da hu	2	2		2
Alab's gr ch	2	8		12
Other	1			2
Total	14	19	11	25

maintain a common hearth. In two instances (the households of headmen *L* and *R*), an *alab* and his younger brother comprised a household with their wives, children, and grandchildren. Another consisted of an unmarried *alab* (*M*), his sister's nuclear family, and some of his deceased brother's children. The other two groups were composed of an *alab*, his nuclear family, and his un-married siblings (the households of *B* and *T*).

The tenth and eleventh households had been formed by quite different processes. Both were joint sibling families which had formed after one of the siblings had been widowed. In one case, the younger brother of *alab A* and his children terminated residence with his wife's household after her death, and he and his children joined *A*'s household which included the latter's wife and his deceased sister's daughter and her children. In the second case, a widowed female and her offspring joined her brother, *alab C*, and his wife to form a household after her husband's death. Both widowed individuals had lost their usufruct rights to their spouses' land when the latter died, and common interest and right to land accounted for their affiliation with a sibling's house-hold.

Table 3.9. Joint Sibling Households

Alab at Head of Household	Alab L Makaoliej M 3/1	Alab R Rinamu R 1	Alab M Makaoliej M 3/2–3/3	Alab B Ijjirik I 2	Alab T Rinamu R 1/1	Alab A Ijjirik I 3	Alab C Ijjirik I 3/1
Alab	1	1	1	1	1	1	1
Alab's mo	1				1		
Alab's wi	1	1		1	1	1	1
Alab's so		2		3	6		
Alab's da	1	4		4			
Alab's da hu		2					
Alab's br	1	1			2	1	
Alab's br wi	1	1					
Alab's br so	3	2	1			1	
Alab's br da		5	3			3	
Alab's br da hu	1	1	1				
Alab's si			1	1			1
Alab's si hu			1				
Alab's si so			1				
Alab's si da			1			1	1
Alab's gr ch	1	4	1	2		5	2
Other	1			1		1	1
Total	12	24	11	13	11	14	7

Districts. The land parcels upon which the households were situated were divided into two districts and three sections. The sections were identified as eastern, middle, and western. Jitoen 'downwind, to the west' district was coterminous with the western section; Jitaken 'upwind, to the east' district included both the middle and eastern sections. Each section was headed by a senior ranking *alab*. The west was headed by *alab A* of Ijjirik lineage I 3, the middle by the head of Makaoliej, and the east by

Plate 6. Bikini woman with her children, 1946. *(Photo by Carl Mydans. Time-Life, Inc.)*

Plate 7. The aged Lokwiar, 1946. *(Honolulu Star-Bulletin.)*

chief Juda. As indicated in Map 5, the ranking Ijjirik males were clustered in the eastern section. Located in this section were the households of Juda, Lokwiar, and *alab B* of Ijjirik lineage I 2.

The sections were units in a distribution system which functioned on those few occasions when the paramount chief sent food or other items from the southern atolls and when the community assembled to feast and observe life crisis celebrations and other important events such as Christian holidays. A good-natured rivalry existed between the sections and districts, and they competed in games and celebrations. The sections also functioned as work units for the accomplishment of a few tasks. The maintenance of the church, school, and council house was the responsibility of all adults, and when any of the buildings were in need of repair, work was allocated among the sections. Few work activities, however, involved the entire community, and none of them required a sustained effort.

Summary

As the foregoing account reveals, rights to land permeated the entire fabric of Bikini society. Although change was occurring prior to relocation as a consequence of the intervention of foreigners, the control and manipulation of rights to a large amount of land provided the basis for the power and influence of the chiefly lineage in the community. The power and influence of other traditional leaders were similarly derived from their authority over the various estates into which the atoll was divided. Ambiguities and alternatives in the rules governing succession to political office and the inheritance of land rights gave the system some flexibility and provided room for individuals and competing interest groups to maneuver as they sought to maximize their own interests. Inevitable consequences of the system were the disputes over land and statuses of power and influence—the source of most of the discord within the small community.

Land rights also exerted a great influence on residential alignments and choices. With only two exceptions, the headmen had their households on land parcels over which they had authority, and the location of the parcels determined the section and district of the settlement to which they belonged. Land rights primarily accounted for the cognatic character and the flexibility of the domestic units as those rights provided a number of alternative choices of residence.

Further, and as described in Chapter Two, the paramount chief's authority over the Bikinians and other islanders within his domain was also rooted in the system of rights to land. Indeed, all of Marshallese society has traditionally been structured in terms of rights to land, and it would seem inevitable that the relocation of any community from its established landholdings would result in significant alterations in those relations between groups and individuals which are either determined or influenced by land rights. Given the competitive nature of the island society when matters of power and land are at stake, relocation is tantamount to the opening of Pandora's box.

CHAPTER FOUR

Rongerik and Kwajalein

The Rongerik Resettlement

Upon their arrival at Rongerik in early March, 1948, the Bikinians found their new village was incomplete, although, a total of twenty-six tent structures, the same number of dwellings that had been abandoned at Bikini, had been prepared by the advance party. In contrast to Bikini's dispersed settlement pattern, the Rongerik village plan, prepared by Americans, resembled a community in the United States—dwellings were arranged in a compact L-shaped cluster on the main island. Before the community was disembarked, the naval officer in charge had Juda go ashore to determine which dwellings were to be occupied by each household (Meade 1946). Perhaps as a result of Juda's hurried, spur of the moment allocation of dwellings, two households which had been adjacent at Bikini were assigned dwellings at opposite ends of the village. Other households which had been adjacent were given dwellings in close proximity to one another. The general composition of ten of the eleven households was preserved, and the eleventh was divided when the widowed brother of *alab A* and his children were given a separate residence. He was to remarry shortly thereafter, and his nuclear family came to comprise a twelfth household. The households were no longer located on parcels of land, however, and this remained the situation for the duration of the settlement; land was never divided on Rongerik.

As the Bikinians settled into their new surroundings, the officer in charge directed their work. Men were given meals and paid

77

a small sum for their labor. It was hoped that this arrangement would give the people a cash reserve and permit direct supervision of their work. With the construction of concrete cisterns, the village was considered virtually finished, and all Americans departed by the end of the month. The Bikinians were left with the task of replacing the canvas coverings of the tent frames with pandanus thatch.

Food provided by the Americans was sufficient for several weeks. The community's small store was well stocked. All tools and surplus materials left from the construction work were given to the Bikinians. They also received a radio receiver and a gasoline generator so they could keep abreast of developments at Bikini. A press release issued by naval authorities reported that the relocation was an unqualified success.

> The Seabees built a model village on Rongerik that anyone would be proud to live in, complete down to Chick Salers of the latest model, which it is hoped the natives will admire and perhaps use. The natives are delighted, enthusiastic about the atomic bomb, which already has brought them prosperity and a new promising future (*Honolulu Star Bulletin,* April 1, 1946, quoted from Mason 1954:283).

The resettlement's initial weeks were something of a honeymoon period. In addition to the American supplied food, the Bikinians collected a rich harvest of coconuts and pandanus from trees which had long been unexploited except by small parties of Rongelabese which had occasionally visited the atoll. As soon as the people began to subsist on local foods, it became apparent that Rongerik's resources had been greatly overestimated, and were, in fact, inadequate. The coconuts were smaller than those to which the people were accustomed, and it was discovered that both the palms and pandanus trees were less productive than those of Bikini. All coconuts were required for subsistence; surplus was not available for copra. The quantity and quality of fish and other marine fauna in the lagoon proved to be poor in comparison to Bikini, and the people learned that certain species of fish which were edible at Bikini were toxic in Rongerik's waters. Consumption of these fish caused stomach disorders, diarrhea, and partial paralysis of the limbs.[1]

Other difficulties were encountered. After exhausting a supply carried from Bikini, the islanders found that the fiber from the husks of Rongerik's coconuts was of such poor quality that it could not be processed into durable sennit. As a result, some dwellings remained unthatched and canoe repairs were not made.

Less than two months after their arrival, the Bikinians expressed anxiety over Rongerik's resources and made the first of their many requests to be returned home. The administration suspected, however, that they were beginning to depend too much upon the government and were not making an effort to adjust to the atoll. This suspicion was reinforced by visitors to Rongerik who reported a lack of activity and enthusiasm. During Operation Crossroads, Rongerik was a side show for Americans involved in the main event at Bikini. Sea planes which shuttled back and forth between Kwajalein and Bikini frequently landed at Rongerik for the benefit of some official party or newsmen. The Bikinians grew accustomed to their visitors and took full advantage of their appearances to exchange handicraft for cigarettes, money, and other items. Such occasions interrupted the islanders' normal routine, and visitors went away with the impression that the people were engaged in little constructive activity. Other evidence indicates, however, that the Bikinians were attempting to extend the planting of coconut and pandanus to increase Rongerik's resource base (Kiste 1968:56).

The administration also feared that ineffective leadership was the source of some of the islanders' troubles. As Juda's succession to the chieftainship had been recent and contested, he suffered under the handicap of his own inexperience, and he probably did not have the support of the faction which had op-

---

[1] This phenomenon is quite common in the Pacific; a species of fish eaten without ill effects in one locale may cause illness, sometimes fatal, in another. There is some reason to believe that the poisoning originates in the diet of fish, but whatever its source, its chemical nature is unknown (Wiens 1962: 292-294).

posed his incumbency. Further, Juda had little experience in dealing with Americans, and it is very likely that he was intimidated by navy officers of high rank. Thus, at a time when he was being heralded by the press as "King of Bikini" and was attempting to cope with problems of a magnitude which no chief before him had ever encountered, he made a poor impression on Americans. He appeared indecisive and " . . . seemed to be confused by the demands made upon him as a leader of the displaced group" (Mason 1954:294).

The Americans did not believe they could simply change the community's leadership, and they became increasingly concerned as the Bikinians continued to experience difficulties and reiterated their plea to return home. In an attempt to convince them that Bikini was unsafe, Juda was flown there after the first atomic test had been conducted on July 1, 1946. The test had been an aerial shot over the lagoon; vessels in the target area had sustained great damage, but there were few visible results on shore. Trees were bearing and appeared unharmed; the danger of radioactive contamination could not be observed, and Juda did not understand its hazards. He returned to Rongerik unconvinced, and the second and final test in Operation Crossroads was conducted on July 25, 1946.

Continued consumption of Rongerik's crops exhausted the supply, and in August, 1946 the Bikinians became alarmed when the palms stopped bearing. This had never occurred at Bikini, and the people reported it to the administration. While the cause of the phenomenon was never discerned, the Bikinians had their own explanation for it and their other troubles. Rongerik had a bad reputation among Marshallese because of its association with Libokra, an evil female *ekejab* 'spirit'. According to myth, Libokra once lived in the southern Marshalls where Rongerik was originally located. She stole the atoll and hid it among the northern islands. Libokra attempted to settle at Bikini, but was driven off by Orijabato, a benevolent spirit who resided there and guarded the Bikinians. Libokra fled and wherever she visited, fish became poisoned and the crops declined. Eventually, she returned to Rongerik where she died. Her body was cast into the lagoon, and those fish which ate it became poisoned and have ever since made people ill when eaten (Erdland 1914:348; Mason 1954:286-287).

Americans were surprised that Libokra had not been mentioned before the relocation. The Bikinians explained that they
had always been concerned with her malevolent influence, and
that on their first day ashore, parents had warned children not to
eat or drink anything until adults had sampled local foods. They
claimed, however, that initially they had considered Libokra to
be relatively unimportant because they had understood that their
relocation was a temporary measure and a short term inconvenience could be endured.

In the following months, the situation worsened. Food shortages occurred during the winter of 1946-47. In May, 1947, all
hope of a successful settlement ended when a fire of undetermined
origin destroyed thirty percent of the trees on the main island and
drastically reduced food supplies. As an emergency measure, the
Bikinians began to make voyages by sailing canoe over the eighteen miles which separated them from Rongelab. Old people and
children were taken to stay with relatives and fellow clansmen,
and the sailors usually returned to Rongerik with food provided
by the Rongelabese (Mason 1948:17).

The situation caused the governor of the Marshalls to appoint
a Board of Investigation composed of three navy officers and one
civilian to evaluate the islanders' plight. The Board convened at
Rongerik in early June, and the people were told that its members
had come ". . . to look at the island and talk about moving" (Records of Proceedings of a Board . . . . 1947). In a session with the
council, chief Juda was questioned; he reported that there was insufficient food, the store was bankrupt, fresh water supplies were
low, and the atoll had only one brackish well. He told the Board
that of several sites which had been suggested for relocation, the
council had decided upon Kili Island. Each *alab* was questioned,
and all affirmed the preference for Kili.

Later in the month, Juda, *alab* B of the second ranking Ijjirik
lineage, Lokwiar's son (the council scribe), and the Makaoliej *alab*
M accompanied the Board on a survey of Kili Island and Ujae and
Wotho Atolls.[2] They examined each as a possible relocation site,

---

[2] As described in Chapter Two, Ujae Atoll was considered as a possible relocation site prior to the Rongerik resettlement. Wotho had not been considered previously. Wotho has thirteen islands with a total land area of 1.67

and the four Bikinians were returned to Rongerik to consult with their fellows and decide upon their first and second choices for a new home. The paramount chief was consulted, and he responded with a document offering the Bikinians land at either Ujae or Wotho both of which were in his domain. On July 25, the Bikinians made a written reply to the military government:

> To the Office at Kwajalein
> From the Council of Rongerik
>
> Gentleman:
>
> I have choosen the place where to go to live on and it is the island of Ebbetyu and Enelamoj (Ujae). These we have all agreed upon.
> But now I have been thinking, since these move will be the last move and the place we go to will be our home forever and ever therefore we wish to be removed to an atoll where there are no other people. These is what we ask of you but we will do whatever you'll say (Ibid.).

During the same month, the Marshalls and other islands of the former League of Nations Japanese Mandate became the United States Trust Territory of the Pacific Islands within the framework of the United Nations Trusteeship Council. The military government was ended, but as an interim measure, the navy was delegated the responsibility for the new civil administration until authority was transferred to a civilian agency. With the creation of the Trust Territory, however, the welfare of the islanders became subject to the scrutiny of international representatives of the Trusteeship Council, and the resettlement of the Bikinians was no longer a matter that could be handled discreetly by agencies of the United States government (Mason 1954:314).

Concurrent with these events, the situation at Rongerik further deteriorated. A medical officer who accompanied a July field trip to the atoll reported that the Bikinians were "visibly suffering from malnutrition" (Ibid.). The council's ambivalent response had not helped solve the problem, and in another attempt to convince the Bikinians that a return home was impos-

---

square miles; its lagoon covers 36.6 square miles. In the latter part of the 1940s, its population was between thirty to forty islanders (Bryan 1972: 142-143; Mason 1954:310).

sible and that it was necessary to make a decision about their future, the governor of the Marshalls flew to Bikini with Juda and the same three Bikinians who had accompanied him on the earlier survey of Kili, Ujae, and Wotho. They spent several days on Bikini in early August, but, as in Juda's previous visit, the administration's idea backfired. Bikini was occupied by a team of scientists involved in the Bikini Resurvey, a two-month long investigation of the effects of the atomic tests. The presence of the researchers suggested to the Bikinians that humans could live on the atoll without harm. Further, more than a year had elapsed since the nuclear tests, and the lagoon's marine fauna appeared healthy and abundant. Unexploited trees were laden with coconuts, and the only change the islanders ". . . professed to notice was the presence of a new plant, papaya, the seeds of which may have been introduced during Crossroads" (Hines 1962:64).

In mid-August, the Board took Juda and the same three men to Ujelang. The atoll is located in northern Ralik (see Map 1, page 10). It had been a commercially operated copra plantation before World War II and had been uninhabited for several years. The Bikinians thought it "nice" and were returned to Rongerik with their observations. On August 26, the people notified the administration:

Gentlemen:

We the council have held a meeting to find the best place to go to. We have been to some other places to inspect and have considered them. In moving we find it quite a problem. The place we all agreed to stay on is Rongerik Atoll (Records of Proceedings of a Board . . . . . 1947).

The civilian member of the Board was replaced by another, an agriculturalist, who conducted a survey of Rongerik, Kili, Ujae, and Ujelang. His report substantiated the Bikinians' reports; Rongerik's resources had grown so low that the islanders had begun cutting down young palms to eat the heart, a progressively destructive procedure which could only reduce future harvests. The agriculturalist described the islanders as a defeated, frustrated, poverty-stricken people who thought of home only as Bikini. In his opinion, their departure from Rongerik had already been too long delayed. He judged Ujelang's resources as adequate and recommended it as the best site for resettlement (MacMillan 1947).

On September 1, the governor and the Board flew to Rongerik to learn why the Bikinians had decided to remain there. They indicated that their primary concern was to return to Bikini, and they could not agree on another relocation site. To them, Ujelang was too distant and lacked pandanus. Wotho was too small; it and Ujae were inhabited, and resettlement on either could result in populations too large for existing resources. Further, the Bikinians wanted to keep their community intact, and they were strongly opposed to residing with another population. Kili, while uninhabited, had no lagoon and was now judged undesirable. They wished to stay on Rongerik because of its relatively close proximity to Bikini, and they reportedly felt obligated to remain because of the village constructed by the Americans. The islanders also feared that the costs and effort required by another relocation might earn them the displeasure of the Americans. The possibility of moving to Ujelang was discussed, and the Americans returned to Kwajalein.

The Board concluded that Rongerik was inadequate and expressed doubt that it could ever produce resources sufficient for the people. The Board's first choice was to return the people to Bikini. Assuming that this was impossible, it recommended resettlement at Ujelang. The governor concurred and determined the feasibility of Bikini's reoccupation. The results of the investigations conducted by the Bikini Resurvey, however, revealed that radiological activity precluded Bikini's habitation by a permanent population for years to come.

In late September, 1947, the Bikinians became pawns in internal squabbles within the United States government. The agriculturalist's report on conditions at Rongerik came into the possession of a Washington, D.C. syndicated newspaper columnist. He, a former Secretary of the Interior and long time critic of the naval island administration, charged the navy with the responsibility for the sorry condition of the islanders. The Bikinians became the subject of newspaper articles and editorials throughout the United States and Europe. As a consequence, public opinion as well as the threat of censure by the United Nations placed considerable pressure on navy officials to rectify the situation.

During the second week of October, Juda and at least two

alab were flown to Ujelang in an effort to persuade them to resettle there.   On October 17, navy officials announced that the
Bikinians were to be moved to Ujelang (Mason 1954:325).   Apparently, the Bikinians had agreed to the move, and on November
22 ten Bikini men and twenty Seabees arrived at Ujelang with
materials to construct a village.   Less than two weeks later, officials in Washington, D.C. advised the administration in the Marshalls that Enewetok Atoll was to be used for a second series of
atomic tests and that its inhabitants had to be moved immediately.   Operations in the Marshalls changed accordingly.   The Enewetok people were moved to Ujelang on December 21; the Bikinians remained on Rongerik.   The governor consulted with Juda
and the council, who reportedly decided that perhaps an adjustment to the atoll was possible after all.   Shortly thereafter, the
High Commissioner of the Territory decided to conduct a com-
prehensive study of the Bikini people to determine the ". . . un-
derlying causes of their apparent discontent" (Richard 1957:525).

Response to Crisis

Leonard Mason, an anthropologist from the University of
Hawaii, was engaged to conduct the investigation.   He and an assistant, Mr. James Milne, an islander of mixed Micronesian/Euro-
pean descent, flew to Rongerik by sea plane on January 31, 1948.
Their arrival coincided with the most critical food shortage yet
experienced.   Only immature coconuts and pandanus fruits were
available.   Arrowroot was exhausted on the main island and nearly depleted on others.   The community's store had only one hundred pounds of flour.   Canoes were in disrepair because of the
lack of sennit and, as a result, fishing was largely curtailed and
the relief voyages to Rongelab had ended.   Adults were even con-
suming small quantities of those fish which were found to have
toxic qualities.

The Communal Organization.   Mason learned that, when
their traditional household and lineage organization had proven
ineffective in coping with the crisis, the islanders had responded
by reorganizing their community into a single cooperative unit.

Plate 8. Chief Juda and his wife in 1946 or 1947. *(U.S. Navy photo.)*

Subsistence activities were coordinated by the council, and men were divided into groups and assigned work on the basis of their expertise at different tasks. The best fishermen fished, some men collected vegetable crops, and the rest worked at other chores. In an effort to conserve and to ensure an equal distribution of food, the gathering of coconuts and pandanus from trees in and about the village area was prohibited without the council's consent. The village was divided into four sections with equal memberships, and each was headed by an *alab*. Juda headed one section, the second ranking Ijjirik *alab* headed a second, and the major *alab* of Makaoliej and Rinamu headed the third and fourth. Food was divided by the council into equal shares for the sections, and the *alab* in charge of each allotted it equally among its members.

The Paramount Chief. Mason's research also revealed that the Bikinians' decisions about another relocation site were shaped by factors unknown to the administration. The Bikinians' resettlement on Rongerik had undermined the paramount chief's authority over them, and a number of islanders were advocating that they should seize the opportunity to terminate their subordinate status to him. As noted earlier, Rongerik was within the realm of another paramount chief who had agreed to the Bikinians' resettlement in his territory. Subsequently, no consideration had been given to the Bikinians' future relationship with either of the two chiefs. The situation was without precedent in Marshallese history; the islanders were residing on one chief's land, and at the same time, they were supposedly the subjects of another.

The deprivations which the Bikinians were experiencing provided grounds for questioning their relations with their own paramount chief. They recalled that it was his responsibility to aid them in a time of need, yet they had received no assistance from him. Some Bikinians believed that the Americans, particularly the navy, should become their paramount chief and had begun to develop a rationale in support of their position.

> After all, they argued, who established a school and medical dispensary on Bikini and provided training for Bikinians to administer both? Who had gone to a great trouble and expense to see that Bikinians were safely relocated on another atoll when Bikini was needed for atomic experimentation? Since the administration had borne all responsibilities once charged to the paramount chief why should the United States not become paramount chief? (Mason 1954:493).

The Bikinians had observed the Americans marshal the manpower and other resources required for Operation Crossroads and their own relocation. The outcome of World War II and the nuclear experiments were still fresh in mind, and the people had clearly concluded that American power and material wealth were immeasurable. It was readily apparent to many that a substitution of the United States for the paramount chief would be advantageous to their own interests and welfare. Other Bikinians, however, feared the paramount chief's magical powers and took a more conservative stance: "We cannot take another (paramount chief) . . . nor break with him, for if we did, something very awful might happen to us" (Ibid.).

Regardless of such differences of opinion, sentiments favoring a separation from the paramount chief had strongly influenced the islanders' earlier inclination to select Kili as a possibility for resettlement. Kili was not part of any chief's domain; it had been a commercially operated copra plantation in Japanese and German times and had passed to the United States as public domain. From the point of view emerging among the Bikinians, the atolls of Wotho, Ujae, and Lae which had been considered for relocation were deemed undesirable not only because of their small size and that they were already inhabited, but they had the additional disadvantage of being part of their paramount chief's domain.

Kwajalein Sojourn

Events of early 1948 strengthened the position of those who desired that the United States become a surrogate for the paramount chief. Three days after Mason's arrival at Rongerik, an officer of the administration arrived and was informed of the situation. A message sent to the governor urged immediate relief measures. Swift action was taken; the following day food and a medical officer were flown to Rongerik. The doctor examined the Bikinians; he pronounced their condition to be that of a starving people. On February 7 the governor arrived and outlined a plan to evacuate the islanders to a temporary camp on Kwajalein until another relocation site could be found. He proposed to subsidize the community and provide employment for those who desired it while on Kwajalein. The Bikinians responded with enthusiasm (Mason 1954:344-345), and they reaffirmed their approval of the governor's scheme when they were visited later in the month by the High Commissioner, an admiral (Richard 1957: 528). On March 14, the Bikinians loaded their possessions and delapidated canoes on board a navy vessel and arrived at Kwajalein the following day. The Rongerik resettlement had lasted two years and one week.

Kwajalein represented a totally alien environment for most Bikinians. They were given refuge on Kwajalein Island, the largest in the atoll, which had been denuded of almost all vegetation by the American invasion force of 1944. The island had a large concrete air strip, quonset huts, a variety of wooden structures, offices, churches, and tents. The lagoon side of the island was equipped with a docking area for vessels and was cluttered with marine equipment. The military community consisted of a few thousand American males and was complete with streets, electric lights, water distilled from the sea, telephones, radios, movie theaters, and a post exchange.

On the island's ocean side was a camp of Marshallese laborers, mostly males, who were recruited from all over the archipelago. Next to the camp, a tent village of three parallel rows of ten closely spaced canvas-roofed dwellings had been constructed for the Bikinians prior to their arrival. The thirty units had corrugated metal walls and wooden floors, and each was equipped with an electric light. The quarters were cramped; each unit was about ten feet square. The arrangement of the village disrupted former residential groups. In some instances, members of a household occupied adjacent quarters, and in other cases, they were forced to separate.

The Bikinians received their meals in a messhall with the laborers. The fare was plain by American standards but appeared extravagant to the Bikinians after their Rongerik ordeal. Menus consisted of rice, canned fish, bread, beef and vegetable stew, canned fruits, milk, sugar, coffee, and tea. Outside the common mess, the Bikinians remained a community separate unto themselves. Facilities were provided for their school, council meetings, and church services.

The administration reported:

> ... that definite psychological scars were left on the people and the first month on Kwajalein was spent chiefly in checking and restoring their health, rehabilitating their clothing and possessions, orienting them to unaccustomed surroundings, and above all, establishing a sense of security and self-respect (Richard 1957:528).

As soon as they were physically able, adults were employed as manual laborers and given tasks related to the general maintenance of the base. With their earnings, they bought clothing and sampled widely from the variety of goods available at the post exchange. Their health improved rapidly, morale soared, and they were reportedly "... profoundly impressed with the cultural accomplishments of the United States—movies, cokes, candy, ice cream" (Ibid.).

In contrast to the period at Rongerik, no serious problems

demanded the council's attention. Official contacts between Bikinians and Americans were frequent, but were largely maintained between chief Juda and the administration (Mason 1954:427). As individuals, the *alab* had little opportunity to exercise any of their traditional authority. The kin groups which they headed were not functional in the alien environment, and the *alab* had little to do with directing the daily activities of the community. Wages meant an unprecedented degree of economic independence for most adults. As the *alab* did not control essential resources, others were not dependent upon them. With meals and housing provided at no cost, workers were free to gratify their own wants. The traditional leaders had no customary rights to others' wages, and three or four of them who were too old for physical labor became dependent upon their younger kinsmen.

The islanders had never been more prosperous in terms of material well-being, and the satisfactions they derived from this aspect of their Kwajalein sojourn helped offset memories of Rongerik. More importantly, the Bikinians were thrust into greater contact with outsiders than at any previous time. Many of the islanders in the labor camp were among the most acculturated Marshallese; some had worked for the Japanese prior to the Americans and preferred salaried employment to life in traditional communities. Contact with the laborers served to both reinforce the negative image the Bikinians had of themselves and expose them to novel viewpoints. Compared to the laborers, the Bikinians were a group of unsophisticates and were reminded of their reputation as a backward people when one or two men from the camp were discouraged by their fellows from marrying Bikini women. At the same time, certain notions that were common among the laborers supported those of the Bikinians who were reevaluating their relationship with the paramount chief. Many laborers took a dim view of the chiefs. As they earned their livelihood outside the traditional economy, they were no longer inclined to accept a status subservient to that of the chiefs, and they questioned the traditional social order which divided islanders into privileged and commoner classes.

Contact with Americans also provided ideological grounds for reevaluating the traditional order. Some navy personnel ridiculed the idea of hereditary chiefs, and officials encouraged the people to run their council in a democratic fashion. Enlisted personnel gave more tangible expression to the ideals which Americans are quick to espouse (if not practice in the United States) and were relatively egalitarian in their behavior and attitudes toward the Marshallese.

Within this social milieu, the Bikinians' paramount chief damaged his own interests. The chief was quite advanced in years, and he was often represented by his heir apparent. The two chiefly men demanded that the Bikinians provide domestics for a household they maintained on Kwajalein. The chief's heir paid frequent visits to the Bikinians and reportedly behaved as if he were a chief with the power and prerogatives of former times. The Bikinians resented the demands made upon them and learned from the laborers that few chiefs dared to act in such an autocratic fashion; they were advised to forget the chief and cast their lot with the Americans.

With the apparent encouragement of the laborers, the Bikinians further developed their rationale for severing their ties with the chief. Some recalled that, unlike their own ancestor Larkelon, paramount chief Kabua of the last century had not conquered Bikini by force of arms, and they claimed that they had never really been subject to him or any of his successors. They also charged that they had been denied medical care in Japanese times because the chief had failed in his obligation to assume the costs. They also found it convenient to recall that the Japanese had claimed the atoll as the property of their Emperor and had terminated whatever rights the chief might have had.

Selection of Kili

The administration began the search for another resettlement site by consulting the Bikinians' paramount chief and the chief who held Rongerik. The choice of sites was narrowed to Wotho Atoll and Kili Island. The paramount chief, not wanting to lose control over the people, urged that they be resettled within his domain on Wotho. He was told to discuss the matter with the Bikinians. The Rongerik chief was excused from further participation in the proceedings as he had interest in neither site.

In April the governor, chief Juda, three *alab*, the paramount chief, and his heir apparent flew to Wotho. Again the Bikinians were not favorably impressed. To them, Wotho was too small, and they had frequently stated that they did not wish to be settled on an atoll inhabited by others. The Wotho survey lasted less than one day.

In May Juda and ten men were taken by vessel to Kili where they were left alone to explore for two weeks. Kili has an elongate configuration with a fringing reef shelf which extends unbroken around its entire perimeter (see Map 6). The island is a little over 1.10 miles in length and averages about one-quarter mile in width. Its area of 0.36 square mile (230 acres) is about one-half the size of Bikini Island and one-sixth of Bikini Atoll's twenty-six islands. In contrast to Bikini, Kili has a rich soil cover. A depression in the island's center contains a humus-laden black muck which forms an excellent taro swamp of about 4.25 acres. Kili's soils and favorable location in the wet belt of the southern Marshalls offer considerable agricultural potential.

The quality and extent of Kili's coconut groves favorably

Plate 9. Aerial view of Kili Island from the west.

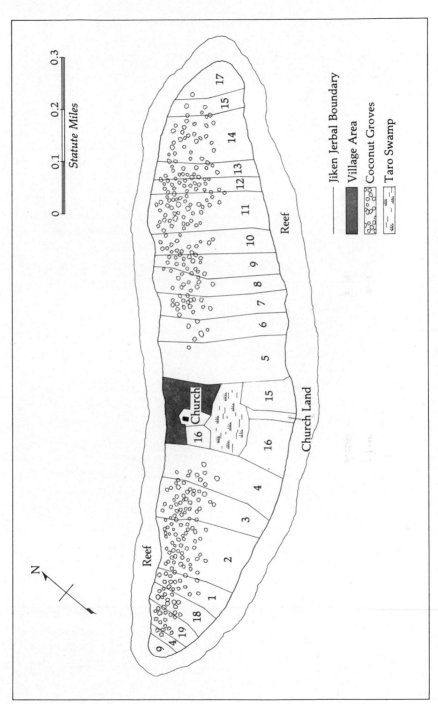

Map 6. Kili Island showing the separate land parcels. *(After a map by Leonard Mason.)*

impressed the Bikinians. The island's development as a copra plantation had begun in the 1870s when a trader purchased it from a paramount chief. Kili passed to German hands, and German, and later, Japanese plantation managers improved the plantation. By the end of the Japanese period, well-ordered rows of excellent quality coconut palms covered ninety-five percent of the island. Few pandanus trees and no arrowroot had been allowed on the plantation. Crops with which the Bikinians had little familiarity—breadfruit, papaya, banana, sweet potato, and taro—remained from the small population of about thirty islanders who had worked as laborers on the island, but these were not sufficient in quantity to support the Bikini community. As Kili had been uninhabited for four years, however, all crops were in maximum abundance when the Bikinians surveyed it.

Kili has great disadvantages. It has neither lagoon nor sheltered fishing area, and the reef shelf offers poor feeding grounds for marine life. The most abundant marine fauna are such deep water fish as tuna and bonito which are found in the open ocean around the island. Kili's long axis tends in an east–northeast to west–southwest direction, which in the absence of a lagoon, is quite unfavorable because it runs almost parallel to the northeast trades. No side of the island can be described as leeward, and there is no protected anchorage for vessels which might otherwise be used for trolling the ocean waters. The worst conditions occur from November to late spring when the tradewinds create heavy surf which isolates Kili and except for infrequent calm spells curtails fishing. In Japanese times, vessels based at Jaluit Atoll thirty miles away took advantage of such calms to make the short run to Kili to load copra and unload supplies. Carving out an existence on Kili is made even more difficult during the winter months when the season of minimal breadfruit yield coincides with the rough seas.

Skills and work habits quite different from those of the Bikinians were required on Kili. To achieve an adequate subsistence level, they would have to rely less on marine resources and take full advantage of the island's agricultural potential. Their casual attitude toward agricultural work would have to be abandoned and they would have to learn and practice the techniques required to cultivate the subsistence crops unfamiliar to them. All of these crops, at least in their immature stages, require more attention and care than do the plants common to Bikini. The cultivation of taro is especially arduous and involves long hours of continuous back-straining labor.

The administration assumed that if the Bikinians were resettled on Kili, the palm groves would yield a coconut crop far in excess of the people's subsistence needs and that this surplus could be converted into copra and a substantial cash income for the purchase of imported foods. At the peak of the copra trade in the late 1930s, an annual average of one hundred tons of copra were produced on Kili, an amount five times greater than the maximum annual yield at Bikini. Officials thought that with efficient planning and management of resources, the Bikinians could store up a quantity of imported food against the winter season when they would be cut off from fishing and the outside world. The Bikinians, however, had little experience in trading and commercial operations and lacked the managerial and planning skills required.

Kili also offered the potential for increased contacts with the Marshallese who had had the longest contact with foreigners. Within a sixty-five mile radius of Kili are the three southernmost atolls of the Ralik chain. As noted, Jaluit, the former capital of the German and Japanese colonial governments, is only thirty miles to the northeast. Ebon, where both missionaries and traders began their activities in the 1850s, is sixty-five miles to the southwest, and Namorik is sixty miles due west. All were served by the southwestern field trip which originated at Majuro Atoll some 170 miles to the northeast in the Ratak chain. During the first years of the American administration, the southern atolls were administered from Majuro and the northern atolls from offices at Kwajalein. In the fall of 1948 Majuro became the district center from which all of the Marshalls were administered.

Thus, if the Bikinians were to make a successful adaptation to Kili, they would have to alter the entire basis of their economic system and acquire new skills and work habits. Further, the Bikinians would no longer be isolated at the farthermost ends of ship routes and distant from the center of government activity. Increased contacts with more acculturated islanders would be inevitable, and the Bikinians would be required to make an adjustment to a new social environment. No one in 1948 appreciated the extent to which the islanders would have to modify their lives if Kili were chosen for resettlement.

The final choice between Kili and Wotho was to be made by a plebiscite of all adults and not by the council which had selected Rongerik. To aid the people, aerial photographs and a summary written in Marshallese outlining the advantages and disadvantages of both sites were posted in their Kwajalein village. The plebiscite was scheduled for May 25, but the people could not make up their minds and asked for a postponement. The day of decision was rescheduled for June 1. The Bikinians sought advice from officials and other Marshallese. The former discussed the two alternatives but stressed that the decision was ultimately theirs. A few Marshallese employed as interpreters felt that Kili was the better choice and they advised the Bikinians accordingly.

The people cast their votes on June 1. Two boxes were placed in a small room—one was labelled Kili and the other Wotho, and each bore a photograph and description of the designated site. Each adult was given a metal tag, entered the room alone, and dropped his or her token into the box of his choice. Kili was chosen by a vote of fifty-four to twenty-two. The factors determining the islanders' choice were the island's coconut groves and that it was outside the jurisdiction of any paramount chief. The paramount chief was displeased with the results as the future of his relationship to the people was uncertain and had not been considered (Mason 1954:355).

The governor deferred any official action until he once again examined the possibility of restoring the people to Bikini. When he assured himself that the evidence was conclusive that they could not return, he recommended their resettlement on Kili. This recommendation was approved by both the High Commissioner and the Secretary of the Navy by mid-August.

Summary and Analysis

For the American administration, the initial relocations of the Bikinians resulted in unanticipated and unwanted consequences. Because of the Americans' own inexperience in Micronesia, they had assumed that the movement of a small population was a relatively simple matter which could be accomplished swiftly, and with little planning or difficulty. The Americans were neither prepared to comprehend the islanders' deep attachment to their ancestral homeland nor were they able to estimate the size of a population which Rongerik or any other atoll could be expected to support. Even if such matters had been understood, there is no reason to assume that they would have been given any priority over the military and scientific concerns of the United States. While local officials in the Marshalls who had the direct responsibility for the islanders' welfare evidenced real concern over the relocated people, there is little, if any, indication that decision makers in the higher echelons of government in far distant Washington, D.C. gave more than passing attention to the plight of the small community. Indeed, effective action to alleviate conditions at Rongerik occurred only after it was evident that the resettlement had totally failed and the actions of the United States in the islands had become subject to the pressures of world opinion and possible censure from the United Nations.

For the Bikinians, the period of their Rongerik and Kwajalein relocations was one of great uncertainty and anxiety. Their limited exposure to the world beyond the boundaries of their own community made them ill-prepared to cope with the circumstances they encountered. None of their leaders had any appreciable experience in dealing with outsiders, and their chief and magistrate was neither experienced nor secure in his status as head of the community. Both factors partially accounted for an absence of decisive and effective leadership during that period.

The Bikinians' refusal to accept fully the possibility that their relocation was more than a temporary measure was derived from their inability to believe or to adjust emotionally to the fact that Bikini could be lost to them forever. They were, however, well aware that their hope of returning to Bikini or their future elsewhere rested in the hands of the Americans. Their own perception of events during the period confirmed their earlier impressions of the scope of American power and material wealth, and caused many of them to conclude that it would be advantageous to have the United States become a surrogate for their paramount chief.

Throughout the period, the Bikinians were disadvantaged in their dealings with the new administration because of factors beyond their own inexperience. Americans were still unfamiliar and imposing figures in the immediate postwar years. In retrospect, it is obvious that the islanders were uncertain as to how they could best manage their relations with the foreigners to achieve their own ends. Fear of incurring the displeasure of the Americans further accounted for their indecisiveness and vacillation at both Rongerik and Kwajalein. Their own selection of Rongerik had proved disastrous, and in large part, the Bikinians' reluctance to select another site for relocation was a consequence of their hope that the Americans would assume responsibility for their future welfare.

Uncertain as to what means were available to them in their early attempts to rid themselves of the paramount chief, the Bikinians turned to their own history to reinterpret past events in ways they hoped would gain the sympathy of the Americans. The islanders' assertion that they had never been subjects of the paramount chief was clearly a reworking of history to provide a rationale for new goals. The allegations that the chief had failed to meet his obligations in the past and that the Japanese had preempted his rights to Bikini contradicted the denial of his former hegemony over them, but nonetheless, both were advanced as further evidence that he deserved no claim to their allegiance, land, or other resources.

Similarly, the Bikinians drew upon mythological accounts of the past to influence Americans. The myth pertaining to Rongerik's contamination by a malevolent spirit was not made known until after the Bikinians had encountered discomfort on the atoll and had become concerned about convincing the administration that the atoll was unsuitable for habitation and they should be returned to Bikini. Had the myth been an important part of their beliefs, it is most unlikely that it would have gone unmentioned prior to their actual resettlement on Rongerik.

One event at Rongerik may have been an attempt by a desperate people to initiate some direct action to end the settlement and effect a return home. As noted, the origin of the fire which destroyed thirty percent of the trees on the main island was never determined. With the possible exception of blazes caused by the

military invasions of World War II, fires of comparable magnitude
are not known to have occurred elsewhere in the Marshalls. Thus,
it seems reasonable to suggest that the Rongerik fire was either
kindled or, more likely, allowed to spread as a dramatic means
of attracting American attention and concern.

Events of the period, however, did provide the Bikinians
with the opportunity to acquire greater experience in dealing
with Americans. The degree and kind of contact with Americans
was different for various segments of the community. All Bikinians observed Americans in the context of official visits and public meetings held to explain administration proposals. Direct intercourse with officials, however, was limited to relatively few
Bikinians. At Rongerik, the members of the council were most
directly involved in the negotiations with officials. At both Rongerik and Kwajalein, four of the councilmen had more extensive
contact with the administration than did their fellows. One of
the four was Juda, who, because of his dual role as hereditary
chief and magistrate, was most directly involved with officials.
He alone was taken to Bikini to view the results of the first nuclear test, he led the contingent of Bikini men who were part of
the survey parties which later examined Bikini and evaluated potential sites for relocation, and he served as the principal link in
the administration's line of communication with the community
at Kwajalein. Juda's conspicuous role not only gave him considerable experience with Americans, but the continued recognition
and support as head of the community by officials as well as his
fame as "King of Bikini" generated by the news media enhanced
his position and provided him with a greater prominence among
his fellows than he had previously enjoyed.

The other three men who played conspicuous roles during
the period were those who accompanied Juda on the second reconnaissance of Bikini and the surveys of potential sites for relocation. Two of the three already occupied prominent positions
in the community and the reasons they were delegated such important responsibilities appear obvious. One was *alab B* who, as
head of the second ranking Ijjirik lineage, was subordinate only
to Juda in the traditional power structure of the community.
The other, Lokwiar's son, the scribe, was second in authority to
Juda within the framework of the council organization. Reasons

for the third male's participation in the survey parties are not so apparent. He, *alab M,* headed the junior of the two large Makao-liej lineages. He had had some brief experience with Americans at Kwajalein after the war (Mason 1954:306), and as a consequence, may have been deemed more qualified than others for the task. Whatever the reasons for the latter's inclusion in the survey parties, all three men who accompanied Juda acquired more familiarity with American officials than their fellows and gained greater influence as important molders of opinion in the community.

With the exception of these four men, most of the traditional leaders experienced some eclipse of their former statuses in community affairs. Perhaps the Bikinians had lost some confidence in their leaders at Rongerik because they had been responsible for selecting the atoll for relocation. More certainly, the Kwajalein sojourn diminished the traditional power and influence of the *alab.* Because they had no authority over resources at the military base, many of their younger kinsmen became economically independent for the first time. In addition, the Bikinians as a group were exposed to both Americans and the Marshallese of the labor camp who openly challenged traditional authority. As a collective body, the council, the *alab,* lost control of community affairs when the administration neither gave them real responsibilities at Kwajalein nor entrusted them with the selection of a site for their third relocation. Thus, by the end of the Kwajalein relocation, there were some indications that alterations were occurring in the traditional power and authority structure of the community.

CHAPTER FIVE

The Kili Resettlement: 1948-1954

Founding the Settlement

In late September, 1948 two vessels carrying an advance party of twenty-four Bikini men and eight Seabees under the command of a navy officer arrived at Kili. Because of rough seas and Kili's reef, the vessels could not be anchored near the shore. Over a period of twelve days, lumber, tarpaper roofing, concrete, tools, and other material for constructing a village had to be ferried ashore by rafts. An area was cleared on the north side of the island where the dwellings of the plantation laborers had formerly stood. During October tent shelters, two concrete cisterns, and four permanent buildings—a store, copra warehouse, medical dispensary, and council house—were erected.

On November 2 two vessels arrived bearing the rest of the community. The islanders had only their personal possessions; their canoes had further deteriorated at Kwajalein and had been abandoned as worthless. Kili's reef again hampered operations; rough seas and hazardous landing conditions allowed only a few people to reach shore, and the vessels proceeded to Jaluit and the shelter of its lagoon. Three days later the seas subsided; the vessels made a dash to Kili, and unloading was completed. On November 11 the vessels and all navy personnel were returned to Kwajalein, except for a carpenter's mate who remained to supervise the construction of permanent dwellings. The Kwajalein episode had lasted a little over seven months.

Among the first tasks confronting the Bikinians were the construction of dwellings, clearing of dense overgrowth that had engulfed the palm groves and taro swamp since their abandonment, and a rigorous program of planting subsistence crops. Building a village came first, and the administration provided two months' food supply to facilitate progress. The people worked hard during the first months on the island as they concentrated on building their new homes. When the carpenter's mate left in May, 1949, a total of thirty-five dwellings, nine more than at Bikini or Rongerik, were completed as well as a church and more cisterns.

A redistribution of power, influence, and privilege that was to occur in the community was foreshadowed as the islanders settled into their new homes. The Americans provided the settlement plan, as they had at Rongerik. Houses were arranged in a compact L-shaped pattern. Most were situated along a main roadway, the long leg of the L, paralleling Kili's north shore for a little over 250 yards. Others were located on the 75-yard short leg of the L, which runs inland at a right angle to the north shore forming the east side of the village. Within the right-angle of the L-shaped village plan is a dune-like structure or hill which rises abruptly to about 40 feet. The church was positioned on the hilltop facing the north shore and the main roadway. A path which runs downhill from the church and intersects the main roadway at a right angle became established as the boundary between the two village districts when the dwellings were constructed (see Map 7).

The houses were built in stages. In the first stage, several were built to the east of the intersection, and this area became known as Jitaken 'upwind, to the east'. In the second stage, a few houses were built in the area west of the intersection, and it became Jitoen 'downwind, to the west'. The procedure was twice repeated until sixteen dwellings were located in Jitaken and eighteen in Jitoen. Another house, the thirty-fifth, was placed on the hill near the church for the pastor (Mason 1954: 451-452).

As the dwellings were completed, Juda and the council allotted them to family units. The factors which determined residential assignments are not certain. In some cases, families

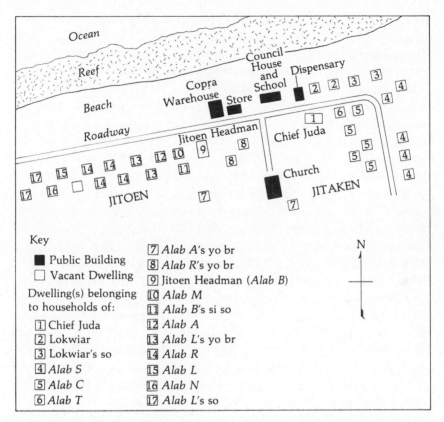

Map 7. Kili village, 1949. (After a map by Leonard Mason.)

which had formerly lived next to one another received adjacent dwellings, and in other instances they did not. In contrast to the eleven households at Bikini and the twelve at Rongerik, seventeen were formed on Kili through the fission of some of the former units.

In part the increase of the number of households could be attributed to the greater number of available dwellings and an increase in the population. The number of Bikinians on Kili in the winter of 1948-49 had grown to 208 (Ibid.:435). Medicines from the dispensary had reduced the high infant mortality rate, and Kili's coconut groves had attracted some of the islanders who had been absent from Bikini in 1946. Most of these returned expatriates had been living at Kwajalein and in the northern Ralik;

none of the large contingent of Bikinians at Ailinglablab were drawn to Kili.

Other factors, however, appear to have been important in establishing the increased number of households. None of the three pairs of brothers who had formed joint sibling families at Bikini reestablished common households at Kili. Other new households were established by Lokwiar's son who had formerly resided with his father, and by two males who had resided with households headed by their wives' fathers.[1] In the past, these men had had no alternative but to affiliate with the household of one of the *alab* since the latter had controlled all land. Residential choices, however, were no longer constrained by considerations of land rights, and the creation of these new households further eroded the traditional authority of the several *alab*.

Changes in residential alignments were also a major factor in the rise to a position of greater importance by Juda's second in command, *alab B,* the head of the second ranking Ijjirik lineage. At Bikini he had been subordinate to Juda for reasons of residence and lineage rank. On Bikini, the households of *alab B* and Juda were in the same district and section, (see Chapter Four and Map 5, page 69) and he had been subordinate to Juda in district, section, and community affairs. In addition to the prominence he had gained because of his role in the surveys of proposed relocation sites, *alab B* had emerged as an important figure in Rongerik overseeing part of the communal distribution system. With the Kili resettlement, he further enhanced his position in community affairs. During the construction of the village, Juda took the first dwelling completed in Jitaken, where Lokwiar was also given housing. Later, *alab B* was established in Jitoen. As the highest ranking Ijjirik male and Juda's heir apparent, as well as on the strength of his forceful personality, he was

---

[1] As described in Chapter Four, the younger brother of *alab A* had established his own household at Rongerik. The other two men who had formerly resided with their elder brothers' domestic groups and became household heads on Kili were younger brothers of *alab L* and *R*. The two males who had resided in households headed by their wives' fathers were one of *alab L*'s sons and one of *alab B*'s maternal nephews. These are reflected in Map 7.

soon recognized as the district's headman. Hereafter, he may be referred to as the Jitoen headman.

Juda headed his own Jitaken district and remained in his dual capacity as chief and magistrate. He continued to function as the community's principal spokesman with outsiders, and in 1949, he was summoned by the administration to represent the Bikinians at a conference of atoll magistrates at the district center at Majuro. By the following year, there was evidence that he was secure in his position as the head of the community; he was elected by his fellows to represent them in the newly created Marshall Islands Congress.[2]

The other two men who had gained importance from their roles in the relocations continued to be prominent in community affairs. During the initial years on Kili, Lokwiar's son remained in the office of council scribe. Afterwards, he voluntarily relinquished the position, and the Makaoliej *alab M* was elected to fill the post. Lokwiar's son remained a man of considerable influence, however; his household was in Juda's Jitaken district, and he served the chief as confidant and advisor.

The First Five Years

The communal organization that had developed at Rongerik continued for the first five and one-half years on Kili. This system was advantageous when concentrated effort was required for the construction of the village. Afterwards, two or three days a week were set aside for communal labor. The council met on these mornings and divided all able-bodied men into groups for clearing brush from the groves, opening trails, weeding the taro swamp, and planting pandanus and breadfruit. Copra making, when scheduled, proceeded throughout the week and was not limited to communal workdays. At the urging of the administration, the lone Bikinian who had long resided on Ebon Atoll returned to the community to instruct the people in the techniques for drying copra in the wetter southern islands.

---

[2] The Marshall Islands Congress began in 1950 as a largely advisory body. In more recent years, it has assumed more legislative functions (see Meller 1969).

Few difficulties and no subsistence problems were experienced during the first months on Kili. Crops were collected and distributed under the council's direction. Local resources, food provided by the administration, and copra receipts were divided among the households in shares proportionate to their relative sizes. In order to provide easier access to the island, a navy demolition team dynamited a shallow channel through Kili's fringing reef a short distance west of the village. Small craft could negotiate the channel when seas were calm, but it proved of little use during rough surf conditions. Nonetheless, all seemed to go well, and officials believed that the resettlement was off to a good start and the problem of providing a secure future for the Bikinians was being resolved.

Plate 10. Channel in the reef which surrounds Kili Island, taken during calm sea and low tide, 1963. *(Photo by author.)*

Plate 11. Bikini men attempting to negotiate the channel during the rough seas of winter months, 1964. *(Photo by author.)*

As at Rongerik, such early optimism was premature: a number of setbacks were soon encountered. A shortage of vessels in the entire Trust Territory caused field trip ships to lag far behind schedule, and the islanders were unable to trade their copra for food and other supplies.[3] When vessels did attempt to call, stor-

---

[3] During the time (more than a quarter century) that the United States has administered the Trust Territory, inadequate funding and poor planning have accounted for the unreliable field trip service in the Marshalls. Some

my weather prevented the pickup of copra. Foodstuffs were extended to the community on credit, and men had to swim the
goods ashore through heavy surf. Copra deteriorated in the warehouse while the store sank into debt.

The second year of the settlement began with a low stock
of food. Rough seas continually hampered the landing of cargo,
and by early 1950, food had become extremely scarce. Few fish
could be caught, and the people subsisted mainly on immature
coconuts. This shortage was not as critical as that experienced
at Rongerik, but the islanders were reminded of their ordeal there
and were distraught at the thought of remaining on Kili.

To help the Bikinians secure more food from the sea, the
administration had the Marshallese at Kwajalein construct six
large sailing canoes to replace those that had been abandoned
there. Two of the canoes were shipped to Kili. Men assembled
one only to learn that during calm weather it was exceedingly
difficult to raise it from the sea and carry it undamaged across
the reef to the beach. In rough weather the task was impossible.
The large craft had no utility on the island; the second canoe
was never assembled, and the other four were never delivered.

The Bikinians learned that the smaller one-man paddle canoes were more practical. Two men could lift one of the small
craft over the reef, and they soon became quite skilled in managing them in all but the worse of surf conditions. Drop-line fishing which had been relatively unimportant in the past replaced
trolling and sailing. This method was less fruitful; since only
tuna and a few other deep water fish were caught. Fishing on
and near the reef with spears, throw nets, and poles and lines
was minimally productive.

The loss of the large canoes and resettlement on a single island altered more than the economic sectors of the Bikinian traditional life style. They missed the diversions and pleasures of
sailing and the relief offered from the monotony of life in a
small community by expeditions to nearby islands. The compact
village area heightened the people's awareness of their reduced
freedom of movement; they complained of their confinement on

---

atolls have commonly not been visited for periods of six or more months;
schedules are uncertain, and no provision is made to ensure that ships will
carry the desired quantities and varieties of trade goods when they do call.

Kili and compared it to a *kalbuj* 'calaboose'. In later years, one of the *alab* expressed his feelings on the matter:

> At Bikini, one could always go to another island, but here it's always the same. Sleep, wakeup, Kili. Sleep, wakeup, Kili. Again, sleep, wakeup, Kili.

The replacement of sailing canoes by paddle canoes also affected patterns of cooperation and the allocation of time and effort given to certain tasks. Men no longer formed the work groups required for the sailing and maintenance of the large canoes. Time and effort formerly devoted to the larger vessels could have been rechannelled toward agricultural endeavors. Such was not the case, however. Discouraged at the prospect of a future on Kili, men were inclined to spend their time discussing the island's limitations and reminiscing about their untroubled past at Bikini.

Concerned about the future of the settlement, the High Commissioner had his staff anthropologist assess the situation on Kili in the late spring of 1950. His report gave no reason for optimism. Outside the village area only several acres of coconut groves had been cleared. Copra production had been adversely affected by the poor condition of the groves and the people's consumption of nuts. Little progress had been made toward the development of other crops. Breadfruit trees distant from the village were engulfed with vines and bearing poorly. The people had made some effort to extend the planting of breadfruit but because of their inexperience with the tree most of their attempts had failed.

The taro left in the swamp from the plantation was found to be largely depleted. The large tuberous roots had been eaten, but little attempt had been made to replant the healthy tops for future crops. A young Marshallese man from one of the southern atolls, who was assigned to the community as a school teacher, had attempted to advise the Bikinians on taro cultivation and developed a demonstration plot which had a healthy stand of taro. The Bikinians had not followed his example, however, and they complained that working in the swamp, digging in the mud, and constant weeding were too great an effort. Further, they resented an outsider, especially a young one, giving advice. The teacher offered no other advice, and the people's attempts to propagate other unfamiliar plants were not successful.

The Bikinians' failure to respond to the teacher's well intentioned effort, and their lack of success in planting could be explained only partially by their casual attitude toward agricultural work and their unfamiliarity with some plants. A more significant factor was their attitude toward Kili and their resettlement. With regard to the island, they were " . . . almost completely and unanimously negativistic" and they were convinced that they had been promised they could return to Bikini if its islands were not "burned up or sunk" (Drucker 1950). It was claimed:

> The Navy told us we could live anywhere, meanwhile on a sand island. The Navy would take care of us, we were told until we went back to Bikini (Ibid.).

The Bikinians had no desire to make a commitment to Kili or to adopt the agricultural techniques which would have enhanced their chances of achieving an adequate subsistence. Only two of the traditional leaders, chief Juda and *alab C,* the Bikinian who had worked on Kili in Japanese times, conceded that the island could be made liveable. Otherwise, the Bikinians presented a "united front" to outsiders. They elaborated upon the negative aspects of the island, its small size, the absence of a lagoon, the reef, and the rough winter surf. Some claims could only be viewed as deliberate attempts to impress the Americans with the difficulty of life on the island; it was charged that it rained too much in the south and that Kili's palms were too tall. Children were taught to parrot: "Kili *enana* (Kili 'is bad')." The people claimed that they had never wanted to resettle on Kili and that the governor of the Marshalls had miscounted the votes cast in the plebiscite. In retrospect, Bikini was remembered as ". . . an oceanic land of milk and honey" as opposed to their calaboose and its problems. A song reflecting their feelings and nostalgia for Bikini had been composed:

> Nothing can be right for me, I cannot be happy.
> As I sleep on my sleeping mat and pillow, I dream
>   about my atoll and its beloved places.
> My dreams remind me too painfully
> About all those places I used to know.
>
> When in dreams I seem to hear the sounds I once knew

My memories make me "Homesick."
It is then that nostalgia overwhelms me and makes me weep
Because it is more than I can stand.
(A translation from Marshallese prepared by P. Drucker for the
naval historian Richard 1957:541.)

It was observed that the communal organization had ceased
to be effective. Council meetings were taking up a good part of
each morning, and the day was well advanced by the time the
work was planned. Some men gave little effort to their assigned
tasks; as shirkers were not penalized by the communal distribution system, they had a negative effect on others.

In part, the inability of the council to direct the community
could perhaps be attributed to the decline of the authority of the
several *alab*. More importantly, however, the islanders had no incentive to make an effort to develop land in which they held no
individual right or interest. In recognition of the situation, the
administration repeatedly encouraged the Bikinians to divide the
land on Kili in the hope that such a measure would cause them
to put forth a greater effort.

To provide some relief from Kili's confinement, to assist the
people's efforts at fishing, and to help them ship copra to the district center, the administration provided a forty-foot converted
whaleboat equipped with engine and sail. It was christened the
Crossroads, and in August, 1950, a group of men were taken to
Kwajalein to sail it to Kili. The Americans assumed that the people, having been sailors in the past, would have little difficulty in
navigating and managing the vessel. The reverse was true. The
Crossroads required different skills and organization of personnel
from those involved in sailing an outrigger canoe. The Bikinians
could manage the *Crossroads'* sailing apparatus, but none were
qualified to operate and maintain a marine engine. In contrast
to the past, when each of the sailing canoes fell under the authority of one of the *alab,* the *Crossroads* belonged to the entire community, and it was uncertain as to who would be charged with the
responsibility of its operation. An old man who had had experience in sailing canoes between northern atolls was named captain
of the vessel by the council. In reality, his authority as master of
the ship was never clearly established, and as one Bikinian later
summarized the situation: "Everyone was telling him to go this

way or that way. We really had too many captains." Further, it
was soon apparent that the captain was not familiar with navigating the waters of the southern atolls. On the ship's maiden voyage, the Bikinians missed Kili altogether and stopped at several atolls before finding the island; similar difficulties were encountered
on other voyages.

The Bikinians did not have the opportunity to develop the
skills required for the vessel's operation. In January, 1951, heavy
surf washed it upon Kili's reef, and it sank with a full load of
copra. The *Crossroads'* loss further convinced the people that
Kili was uninhabitable. The communal effort became less effective; the islanders' morale further declined, and they were disturbed
when a change in the administration of the Trust Territory occurred in 1951. The navy relinquished control of the Territory
to the Department of the Interior, and civilians replaced navy personnel. The Bikinians feared that the navy which had relocated
them had now deserted them, and they were displeased when the
new officials attempted to convince them that they had no alternative but to commit themselves to the development of Kili.

The Bikinians did not respond to such prodding, however,
and even when they made the effort to produce copra, their
work often went unrewarded. Hampered by a continued shortage of vessels, the administration could not maintain regular field
trips, and rough seas prevented adequate servicing of Kili when
ships did call. On more than one occasion from 1951 to 1953,
food supplies ran critically low. Copra continued to deteriorate
in the warehouse, and the community's store sank further into
debt. At one time, the situation became so critical that an air
drop of emergency rations was required (Leysne 1952).

Many of the islanders who had been absent from Bikini in
1946 and had joined the community for the Kili resettlement departed for Kwajalein or other atolls where they had been residing.
Some other individuals who had not had much experience away
from home also sought occasional relief from Kili by travelling to
Kwajalein and joining the ranks of the laborers.

In 1951, the need for additional space by the military at
Kwajalein had required the relocation of the Marshallese laborers
to Ebeye Island, three miles distant from Kwajalein Island in the
atoll (Richard 1957:556-565). Laborers were shuttled back and

forth between the two islands by vessel each day, and an urban
shanty town of the laborers' families began to develop on Ebeye.
The Bikinians who travelled there renewed acquaintances with
some of the islanders they had met in 1948, and a few began to
spend most of their time in the new community. Most Bikinians,
however, returned to their relatives and community after an absence of a few months. All who journeyed to Kwajalein, however, witnessed the changes that were occurring there. The temporary structures which had been constructed on the military
base during the immediate postwar years were being replaced
with larger and more permanent facilities. The base was being
expanded, and such luxuries as swimming pools and a small golf
course were added. Kwajalein Island was in effect being equipped
with some of the amenities of suburban America, and all that the
Bikinians saw further convinced them of the magnitude of American power and wealth.

The majority of Bikinians, however, remained on Kili, and
during the first years there they tended to remain with'drawn and
unto themselves. The rough seas which isolate the island during
half of each year hampered intercourse with the outside world.
More importantly, the people were inclined to remain aloof from
their new neighbors because of their own negative self-image and
lack of self-confidence. Initial contacts with the people of Jaluit
reinforced the Bikinians' tendency to remain to themselves. Several who had visited Jaluit on the *Crossroads* had been mildly ridiculed for their unsophisticated ways, and that experience did nothing to improve their self-image.

As the Bikinians on Kili continued to experience discomfort
and deprivation, they became convinced that they had suffered a
great injustice and were being neglected by those who were responsible for their plight. Because of their felt wrongs, they concluded that it would not only be advantageous, but also morally
proper that the Americans provide for them. They maintained
their united front in their dealings with Americans. They continued to elaborate upon the disadvantages of Kili, and frequently
recalled promises to protect their health and welfare that purportedly had been made by navy officers. Their desire to be provided
for contributed to their unwillingness to expend the effort to at-

tempt an adjustment to Kili; this lack of effort contributed to
their discomfort, and the latter reinforced their negative attitude
toward Kili and their desire to receive aid. Their experience with
Americans and the observations of those who journeyed to Kwajalein further convinced them of what they had already concluded:
in terms of the resources at the command of the Americans, it
would be but a small matter for the United States to provide for
all their wants and spare them from further hardships.

The Allocation of Land

Concerned with the Bikinians' failure to adjust to Kili and
their desire to become dependent upon the government, the administration renewed its attempts to persuade them that they
had no alternative but to remain on the island and that it would
be to their own advantage to allocate land. The Bikinians, however, continued to resist such pressures for reasons that concerned
their relations with the Americans, the paramount chief and internal community affairs. First, they feared that a land division
would be interpreted by the Americans as a sign that they were
resigned to Kili. Secondly, uncertainties over the island's legal
status and the paramount chief were yet unresolved. Since the
Bikinians' resettlement on Kili, the paramount chief and his heir
apparent had been lobbying to convince the administration that
they should receive title to Kili as compensation for their loss of
Bikini. Such an arrangement would have perpetuated the Bikinians' status as their subjects and would have entitled them to a
share of Kili's copra. On one occasion, the heir apparent visited
Kili. He was given a polite but cool reception. He was not offered the traditional tribute and was informed by Juda and the
other *alab* that neither he nor the paramount chief were welcome
on Kili. The people were unanimous, and earlier reservations
that had been harbored by some Bikinians about ending their relationship with the chief had now disappeared. They did not
want to share Kili's copra with him, and they knew he had neither the power nor the resources to assist them in any substantial way or restore them to Bikini. They made their position

quite clear to the administration and took advantage of every opportunity to request formal severance of their relationship with
the chief (Mason 1954:494).[4]

Regardless of the uncertainties of the situation and their
overt resistance to American efforts to bring about a land division on Kili, the Bikinians had in fact been considering the matter since the early months of their resettlement. In marked contrast to the united front they presented to outsiders, the islanders were deeply divided over the allocation of land. Most if not
all adult males participated in numerous, lengthy discussions on
the subject. All of the former dissatisfactions and grievances over real and/or alleged inequities in landholdings were revived; and
Kili's small size exacerbated this concern with land.

The eleven *alab* were primarily concerned with how much
land they would control, and displayed little appreciation that
Kili's agricultural potential was greater than comparable tracts
of Bikini land. Those *alab* who had formerly had authority over
the largest estates had a vested interest in perpetuating old disparities, and they wanted the lion's share of Kili. Other *alab,*
however, were taking advantage of the opportunity created by
relocation in order to attempt to gain a greater share of land
than they had previously enjoyed. At one point, it was suggested that Kili be divided into two sections, one for those *alab* who
had had the largest Bikini estates and one for those who had had
less. The proposal was acceptable to no one since no two *alab*
could agree to share authority over the same land.

In their preoccupation over the amount of land each would

---

[4] Navy officials attempted to resolve the issue pertaining to the paramount
chief before turning the Territory over to the Department of the Interior.
Officials drafted an agreement which gave the paramount chief and the Bikinians joint title to Kili in exchange for all of their rights and claims to Bikini. As the agreement recognized the traditional rights of both parties, it
would have perpetuated the Bikinians' subservient status to the chief. The
document was signed by the chief, five of the Bikini *alab,* and four other
men whom navy officers claimed were lawful representatives of other *alab.*
The majority of the *alab* did not sign, and the Bikinians later claimed that
those who did had acquiesced under heavy pressure exerted by the Americans. Navy officials considered the matter closed, but the subsequent civilian administration did not recognize the agreement as legitimate and bind-
ing.

receive, the *alab* gave little or no consideration to what kind of groups would be allotted land. Although they may have been unaware of it, traditional Bikini landholding groups could not have served for the division of Kili. Some islanders had belonged to two corporations, that is, they had been members of both a corporate lineage and a patri-centered corporation; whereas others had only belonged to one corporation, their lineage. It is certain that individuals of the latter category would not have agreed to a land division among both the lineages and the patri-centered groups as such an allocation would have perpetuated the advantage some individuals had formerly enjoyed when they belonged to both types. Similarly, the *alab* and the other members of the patri-centered corporations would not have agreed to a division of land only among lineages.

Thus, for a land division to occur, discrete groups of individuals had to be delineated, and a reorganization of the community was inevitable. That new groups had to be formed became apparent to the Bikinians when several of the men who had established households of their own on Kili demanded to become *alab* in their own right with authority over land. They refused to have their subordinate statuses perpetuated, and some threatened to leave the community if their ambitions were not realized.

During the first five years on Kili, disagreements over land within the community and the islanders' concern over their relations with the paramount chief and Americans precluded any decision or action. Sometime during this period, Lokwiar and *alab* S of the junior Rinamu lineage R 2 died. As both were heads of patri-centered corporations and were without matrilineal heirs, their eldest sons were recognized as their legitimate heirs and successors as *alab* on their Bikini lands. On this basis, both sons succeeded their fathers as members of the council.

Several events coincided in 1953 and early 1954 to precipitate a land division. In the summer of 1953, the administration changed its position about the finality of the Kili resettlement when it considered the possibility of moving the Bikinians to the small uninhabited atoll of Erikub in the northern Ratak (see Map 1, page 10). The atoll was examined by a party of Americans, chief Juda, and several of the *alab*. They were unanimous in opinion; Erikub was less adequate than Rongerik. With no prospect of another resettlement, the Bikinians resumed their deliberations over dividing Kili. The communal system had completely failed. No one was content with it; men had ceased to cooperate with the council, and they wanted land of their own free from the council's supervision.

In an attempt to salvage the settlement, the administration initiated the Kili Development Project. The community development officer in charge of the project was Mr. James Milne, the islander who had accompanied Mason to Rongerik in 1948. Milne had been attending the University of Hawaii, and in preparation for his assignment he studied tropical agriculture and community development under Mason's supervision. He arrived at Kili in February, 1954 to reacquaint himself with the people and familiarize himself with the task that lay ahead. He observed the failure of the communal effort and encouraged the people to establish separate landholdings. In April, he left to confer with administration officials. By the time he returned the following month, a land division had been accomplished.

A New Scheme of Landholding. After all else had failed, Juda had devised a scheme for the land division. He proposed that households be allotted land in proportion to their relative sizes. The members of each household were to receive land as a group; neither lineage membership nor membership in the former patri-centered corporations was considered relevant for the division of Kili.

Allotting land to households was a qualitatively new idea. As described in Chapter Three, landholding corporations had been composed of either one of two sets of consanguines: a lineage composed of kinsmen related through matrilineal descent or a patri-centered group composed of a male and his own children. The head of either type of corporation was an *alab* with the headman's rights, and all other members had possessed worker rights to its land. In contrast, the households were flexible units which included various combinations of matrilineal, agnatic, and affinal kinsmen who shared everyday domestic tasks and functioned as a common unit of consumption.[5]

---

[5] Agnatic refers to the tracing of kin relations through males only.

While no household had ever been a corporation, all members of a household at Bikini had had rights to the land upon which it was located, and those rights were clearly differentiated. Members of a household who were also members of the corporation which held the land upon which the household was located possessed either *alab* or worker rights to that land. Other household members possessed the usufruct rights which were extended to spouses, adopted children, and the children of male members of a lineage. Because all members of a household had had some right to the land upon which they had resided, they were accustomed to working as a collective unit on it. In this respect, Juda's idea of allotting land to households bore a certain resemblance to the past: members of each household were to receive land which they could work as a group. A very important difference from the past, however, was that Juda's scheme did not make any distinction among the rights of the various members of the household groups on Kili. With the exception of the males who were to head the groups, all household members held equal rights to the land it was allotted.

While it may be assumed that Juda, as the head of the community, was concerned with finding a solution to the problems which confronted the people, his idea for allotting land was quite compatible with his own interests. As the last representative of his own lineage, Juda had no special desire in reestablishing lineages as landholding corporations. His household was one of the larger, if not the largest, in the community at the time, and according to his plan, he stood to gain control over a proportionately large share of land. Further, Juda's household included all of his own children with whom he had formed a patri-centered corporation at Bikini, and thus, he would continue to hold land with them as he had in the past.

Juda served as the advocate for his plan. The way in which Juda persuaded others to accept this scheme and his management of the negotiations required for its implementation reflected his development as a leader and the influence achieved since he succeeded to office. Juda approached the several *alab* informally and individually to argue that a land division was necessary because of the people's discontent with the communal system, and of the likelihood that they would remain on Kili. After he had

persuaded a majority of the *alab* to accept his plan, Juda presented it in a meeting of the council. The proposal was accepted
with the first of several modifications that were to occur before
it was finally implemented: some Bikinians who were not resident
on Kili were to be counted with the households of their relatives.

Juda and the council directed the land allotment, but it was
accomplished with considerable difficulty. Fifteen separate households were recognized in the original division. Each of two of the
seventeen households which had been established in 1948-49 had
either fused with another or was counted as a single unit with another for the purpose of the division. Eleven of the fifteen units
were headed by the eleven Bikini *alab* (including the sons of Lokwiar and Rinamu *alab* S who had succeeded their deceased fathers). Four others were headed by men who were either younger
brothers or maternal nephews of *alab*. In addition, it was decided
to establish two other separate parcels of land, one for the church
and another for the members of the small Makaoliej lineage segment M 3/3 who had left Bikini in Japanese times. Its only male
member, male *q* (Figure 2, page 44), had rejoined the community
on Kili.

Juda's plan was further modified as it was implemented.
Initially, Juda and the council determined the number of islanders who were to be included in each group, and several changes
in group affiliation occurred before land was allotted. At their
own request, four or five men were counted with their fathers'
households rather than with the households of their wives' parents where they were actually residing. Because of young children's habit of moving among the residences of real, adopted,
and classificatory parents, it was necessary to define in which
group they would be counted. With few exceptions, children
were included with the groups of their biological parents.

The inclusion of relatives not actually resident on Kili was
not conducted in a systematic manner and probably precipitated
attempts by some to swell the size of their groups by adding ab-
sentees. With one or two possible exceptions, all individuals who
had participated in the Kili resettlement at one time or another
were counted as members of one of the households for purposes
of the division. In a few instances, several islanders who had
been absent from the community since Japanese times were in-

cluded, while most absentee members of the lineages indigenous to
Bikini and their spouses and children from other atolls were not.

Division of Kili. Difficulties were encountered when land
was actually divided. First, an attempt was made to allow the
heads of the various groups to select their own locations on the
island. This failed because all sections of Kili were not of equal
quality, and many wanted land close to the village. One area in
the western part of the island that had been replanted in the late
1930s was especially desirable because its young palms had only
recently matured. Several *alab* laid claim to the section, and for
a time, the land division was in danger of failure because of the
contest which followed.

All the factors which determined the eventual allocation of
land are unknown, but enough data are available to outline the
general course of events. Only three or four *alab* acquired sections of the island they desired. Others who failed to secure
better sections of land chose allotments partly on the basis of
their propinquinty to those of relatives. Factors of kinship, however, were secondary in determining the choice of land parcels.

The contest over the recently planted area in the western
portion of the island was finally decided in favor of the strong-
willed Jitoen headman. The head of the Makaoliej sub-clan, who
had been one of the contenders, then demanded an area in the
eastern part of the island which he considered second best. By
agreeing to Juda's plan, he had relinquished his former status as
a large landholder, and it was feared that he would hold up the
land division if he were denied his second choice. Others yielded
to his demand, and it appears that he was placated in another
way: he was allowed to count more absentee relatives as members of his group than did any other *alab,* and he thereby increased the size of his allotment.

The land division was continued in the western portion of
Kili. The well ordered rows of palms provided a convenient
measure of acreage and were tallied against the number of people in each group. A number of acres at the island's western-
most end were not allotted in the initial division: the palms
there were old and relatively poor, and the extreme end of the
island was covered with marginal brush.

The Bikinians adopted the term *bamli* 'family' to refer to each of the landholding groups; they and the land allotments are numbered according to the order in which the majority were established (see Map 6, page 93).

The first allotment was considered undesirable because of its distance from the village, but it was accepted by *bamli* 1 headed by male *o* (Figure 2, page 44), the elder of the two younger brothers of the head of Makaoliej sub-clan. The area to the east of it was the highly prized section acquired by the Jitoen headman who headed *bamli* 2. Moving still further east, *bamli* units 3 and 4 headed by *alab N* (Makaoliej M 2) and *alab R* (Rinamu R 1) were allocated land before the taro swamp was reached.

The swamp and the coconut groves to the northwest and south of it were skipped over, and the division was continued on the village's east side. The members of *bamli* 5 headed by the son of the deceased *alab S* (Rinamu R 2) whose dwellings formed the eastern border of the village were successful in acquiring land adjacent to their residences. Continuing east, *bamli* 6 headed by *alab T* (Rinamu R 1/1) was established. *Bamli* units 7 and 8 were allotted adjacent holdings at their request; *bamli* 7 was headed by *alab A* (Ijjirik I 3) and 8 was headed by his eldest sister's son, *alab C* (Ijjirik I 3/1). The two men had had their households on the same land parcel at Bikini and desired adjacent holdings on Kili.

For similar reasons, *bamli* units 9, 10, and 11 were assigned adjacent holdings. *Bamli* 9 was headed by *alab M* (Makaoliej M 3/2), and *bamli* 10 by his maternal nephew, the son of the deceased Lokwiar. Both men requested land next to that of *bamli* 11 which was the parcel that *alab L,* the head of Makaoliej sub-clan had demanded.

Moving further east, *bamli* units 12 and 13 were given adjacent parcels because of a former arrangement which had existed between their members at Bikini. *Bamli* 12 was headed by the only male of the small Makaoliej lineage segment M 3/3, male *q* (Figure 2), and *bamli* 13 was headed by one of the two maternal nephews of the Jitoen headman, male *c* (Figure 1, page 43). Male *q* and the wife of *c* were classificatory siblings; the latter had been adopted by the former's mother. When the members of Makao-

liej M 3/3 had left Bikini years before, they had made *c* and his
wife the custodians of the land to which they had held rights,
and because of this former arrangement, the two groups requested
adjacent parcels on Kili.

The division progressed to the island's eastern quarter where
Juda's *bamli,* number 14, received a tract of land. Compared to
other sections, the area was of relatively poor quality, but Juda
accepted it as a compromise to pacify those who believed they
had made a sacrifice by accepting his plan.

Two more groups and the church were yet to be provided
for. *Bamli* 15 headed by male *u* (Figure 3, page 45), the younger brother of *alab R,* the head of Rinamu sub-clan, was given a
narrow strip east of Juda's. The extreme eastern end of the island was poor land like the western end and was also left unassigned. The final allotments of the initial division were made in
the areas near the swamp which had been bypassed. *Bamli* 15
received additional land south of the swamp. *Bamli* 16 headed
by male *d* (Figure 1), the second maternal nephew of the Jitoen
headman, received two small parcels, one south and one northwest of the swamp. A small section south of the swamp was set
aside as church property.

Soon after the division, three men who had been included
in the *bamli* of an elder brother or maternal uncle came forward
and demanded land of their own. They argued that other men
of their status had become *alab* with authority over land as a consequence of the division and saw no reason why they should be
treated differently. Their demands resulted in the fission of certain of the original groups and the creation of three more.

Bamli 7 headed by *alab A* of the junior Ijjirik lineage had
included his younger brother, male *a* (Figure 1), who had been
his ardent supporter in the earlier dispute over the chieftainship.
On Kili, however, the younger brother objected to sharing land
with his elder brother, and he claimed that the original arrangement was unjust because his family of married children with
spouses and children of their own constituted the majority of
the *bamli* while his brother had only a spouse and adopted child.
A series of bitter quarrels ensued. The elder brother was quite
aged by 1954, and he apparently had neither the strength nor
determination to withstand his brother's aggressive behavior. He

withdrew from the *bamli,* and Juda arranged for him and his small nuclear family to take the poor section of unassigned land at the island's eastern end; they became *bamli* 17.

Bamli 1 headed by male *o* (Figure 2), the elder of the two younger brothers of the head of Makaoliej also became divided. Included in the original unit was the youngest of the three brothers, male *p,* a widower. The latter had been absent from the island at the time of the division, and upon his return, he persuaded his brother to divide the allotment. The matter was resolved peaceably, and the younger brother took the western portion of the land. He and his sons became *bamli* 18.

A maternal nephew of *alab A* was the third and last male to acquire the status of head of one of the new landholding units. Informants are not in agreement as to which unit he was first included. It is known that he, male *b* (Figure 1), informed the council that under no circumstances would he remain subordinate to any of the *alab,* and he voiced the familiar threat of leaving the community if his ambition was not realized. Juda arranged for him to have a portion of the poor land west of allotment 18. He and his nuclear family comprised *bamli* 19.

The small section of land at the western tip of the island remained unassigned. The heads of *bamli* units 4 and 9 laid claim to it by contending that they had not received enough land; the section was divided between them. All coconut land had then been allotted; only the swamp and the village area remained communal land.

As the above description reveals, Juda's idea to divide land among households, a rather simple and uncomplicated scheme as originally conceived, was extensively altered in the process of its acceptance and implementation. The resulting nineteen *bamli* landholding corporations were not households but were units whose memberhsip had been largely determined by households as they existed at one point in time. Alterations in group affiliation for the purposes of landholding and the inclusion of some absentee Bikinians had transformed the nineteen *bamli* into new units which differed in composition from the households.

The male head of each of the *bamli* was recognized as an *alab in brij* 'head of land'. As in the past, each *alab* had authority over the land and the people who had rights to it, that is, the members of his *bamli*. Following the traditional practice, each *alab* supervised the collection and distribution of resources on the land and was entitled to one-quarter of the money earned from copra produced from it. A clear distinction, however, was made between two categories of *alab*. The eleven men who had authority over Bikini land were still thought of as Bikini *alab* in contrast to the eight men who had become *alab* only because of the division of Kili. In order to distinguish them from the former, the latter were referred to as Kili *alab*.

Having allocated land, the Bikinians unsuccessfully attempted to conceal what they had accomplished because they still feared that the Americans would assume that they had abandoned their hope of returning to Bikini and were prepared to remain on Kili. They attempted to camouflage the new land allotments by coining the term *jiken jerbal* 'place of work' for each of the land parcels and they did not refer to them by the traditional term, *wāto* (Tobin 1954:14).

Summary and Analysis

Intra-community Affairs. The power structure of the Bikini community was significantly altered during the initial years of the Kili resettlement. Juda, his heir apparent, and the other two men who had gained influence from their roles in the relocations continued to capitalize upon their increased prominence in community affairs.

Most significantly, during the period from 1948 to 1954, both Juda and his heir apparent broadened their bases of power and influence. As at Rongerik and Kwajalein, Juda further enhanced his own position by capitalizing upon continued support from the administration. In addition, as Juda gained experience, there were indications that he had acquired the confidence and support of a larger number of his fellow islanders. His election to the Marshall Islands Congress early in the resettlement was one indication of his increasingly secure position in the community. His incumbency as a Congressman served to heighten his stature among his fellow Bikinians by providing him with the opportunity to acquire more expertise in dealing with Americans and by bringing him into contact with other Marshallese political leaders. Juda's role in the land division was a clear manifestation of his expanded influence and revealed that he himself was now confident and secure in his position at the helm of the community. The status of Juda's next in command, the head of the second ranking Ijjirik lineage was also greatly enhanced by the realignment of residential units on Kili. He maneuvered himself into the position of head of Jitoen, one of the two districts into which the village and community were divided.

The other two men, Lokwiar's son and the Makaoliej *alab M,* achieved no dramatic increase in their spheres of influence, but they did maintain the prominent positions that they had gained. As noted, Lokwiar's son served as Juda's confidant and advisor, and *alab M* succeeded him as council scribe when he relinquished the office.

In contrast, the power and influence of the other Bikini *alab* were further diminished during the period. The Kili land division brought about a major redistribution of power when eight men, the Kili *alab,* took full advantage of the occasion to achieve statuses as headmen with authority over land and people. As the foregoing description and Figures 1, 2, and 3 reveal, these eight were members of four of the five Bikini corporate matri-lineages, and six of them ranked immediately below the heads of the four lineages, that is, they were either second or third in rank and line of succession to the lineage heads. Four were the only younger brothers of the heads of three of the lineages (Ijjirik I 3, Makaoliej M 3/1, and Rinamu R 1), and two were the only maternal nephews of the head of the fourth lineage (Ijjirik I 2) who had no younger brothers. Thus, they advanced their ambitions from positions of strength and influence that were second only to the Bikini *alab* in the traditional structure of the community.

The remaining two men who became Kili *alab* were of a more junior rank within the lineages and they achieved their new statuses by other means. They had been absent from Bikini since Japanese times and were among these expatriates who had returned to the community on Kili; both had viable alternatives to remaining on Kili if their ambitions were not realized, and consequently, it appears that they were more forceful in exerting their demands than would have been possible for other males of comparable status.

One of the two, Kili *alab b* of the Ijjirik lineage I 3, was the lone Bikinian who had long resided on Ebon Atoll and had returned to the community at the urging of the administration. He adamantly rejected any affiliation with any of the Bikini *alab* after the initial land division and was prepared to return to Ebon with his spouse if his wishes were denied. As Figure 1 suggests, he had few close relatives to call upon for support, and his success appears to have been the result of his own intransigence.

The second male, Kili *alab q* of the small Makaoliej lineage segment M 3/3, was not only of quite a junior status, but he was also relatively young. He had experience as a wage laborer at Kwajalein, however, and he felt no insecurity about returning there if his ambitions were not realized. He was strongly supported by Kili *alab c* because of the kin ties between them and the fact that *alab c* and his wife had been the custodians of the Bikini land to which *alab q* and his small lineage segment had rights. *Alab c* and his wife had every reason to assume that the arrangement would be renewed on Kili if *alab q* were to again leave the community, and thus it was in their own best interests to support his cause.

Not obvious from the description of the land division, two males of the fifth Bikini corporate lineage (M 3/2–3/3) also achieved status as *alab* independent of their lineage head, *alab M*. These two were sons of the deceased Lokwiar and of *alab S* of Rinamu R 2 and had succeeded their fathers as Bikini *alab*. Their succession to statuses of Bikini *alab* had entitled them to head *bamli* units of their own, and thereby they had become *alab* with authority over land for the first time.

Thus, as a consequence of the land division, the younger brothers and maternal nephews who had been the immediate heirs and successors to the *alab* of the five Bikini corporate lineages and two men of a more junior rank had become *alab* with authority over land on Kili. All nineteen of the *alab* are listed in Table 5.1 where the kin ties between the Kili and Bikini *alab* are also indicated.

External Affairs. The Bikinians' responses to the initial years of their resettlement on Kili also produced some alterations in the management of their relations with the administration and the paramount chief. Their experiences on the island

Table 5.1. Bikini *Alab* and Kili *Alab*

Lineage	Bikini *Alab*	Successor to Bikini *Alab*	Kili *Alab*	Relationship to Bikini *Alab*
I 1	Juda			
I 2	B		c	B's si so
			d	B's si so
I 3	A		a	A's yo br
			b	A's si so
I 3/1	C			
M 2	N			
M 3/1	L		o	L's yo br
			p	L's yo br
M 3/2–3/3	M	Lokwiar's so		M's si so
		Alab S's so		M's si so
			q	M's si so
R 1	R		u	R's yo br
R 1/1	T			

further convinced them that dependency upon the Americans was their only hope for a future free from hardship. Their observations of the transformations of the military base at Kwajalein and the welfare measures implemented in their behalf reinforced their evaluation of the magnitude of American power and wealth, and of the potential advantages of developing a stance of complete dependence upon the United States. The belief which clearly emerged during the early years on Kili, that they had suffered a great injustice convinced the Bikinians that the Americans were morally obligated to them and gave them additional rationale in support of their goal to have the United States become a surrogate for the paramount chief. As the earlier reservations held by some Bikinians about severing their relationship with the paramount chief were dissipated, the islanders united to form a common front in matters pertaining to the chief and the administration. The paramount chief's heir presumptive was publicly rebuffed, and the Bikinians took advantage of every opportunity to advance their cause with the Americans. Promises to protect and care for their welfare, allegedly made by navy officials, became an integral and routine element in the islanders' appeals to the administration. They elaborated on the negative aspects of Kili and, as at Rongerik and Kwajalein, they reinterpreted both past events and those associated with their relocations to support their aims.

CHAPTER SIX

The Kili Development Project

Launching the Project

The immediate consequence of the land division—that each of the *bamli* began to clear its land and produce copra—was precisely what the administration had desired. The islanders' response also helped to launch the Kili Development Project on a positive course. As defined by the Americans, the project's goals were to: (1) clear the coconut groves of brush and increase copra production; (2) provide instruction in agricultural techniques; (3) stimulate the production and sale of handicraft; and (4) develop a cooperative to manage trading operations. Mr. Milne, the project manager, had two assistants: a man from Kusaie in the Eastern Carolines who was a taro specialist and a Marshallese woman skilled as a handicraft instructor.

Milne soon developed a good personal relationship with Juda who encouraged his people to work with the project team. In cooperation with the council, Milne organized, scheduled, and supervised work activities. Taro, banana, pandanus, breadfruit, papaya, and sweet potato cuttings were imported from Kusaie Island and Ebon and Jaluit Atolls. Men were organized into work teams and began to develop the taro swamp. Milne and the Kusaien taught them how to plant, mulch, and care for unfamiliar crops. The most productive methods of coconut palm cultivation were also introduced; the Bikinians were instructed in the reasons and necessity for keeping the groves free of brush, and they learned why the proper spacing of trees ensured a maximal yield.

Within five months, substantial progress was evident. The

anthropologist, Saul Riesenberg, visited Kili in June, 1954, and reported ". . . it is obvious that the people have worked hard under the manager's direction, and the results are obvious to the eye everywhere" (Riesenberg 1954). Part of the swamp was cleared and planted. The planting of other crops was greatly increased. For the first time, a number of people, including Juda and three or four of the Bikini *alab,* indicated they were willing to remain on Kili if progress continued to be made.

The majority of the islanders, however, remained pessimistic. At least three of the Bikini *alab* withheld their support and led a group of dissidents which dampened the morale and optimism of others. The dissidents were skeptical and critical of efforts to improve their lot on Kili. From their point of view, the success of the relocation was the Americans' responsibility, and the United States owed them wages for their work with the project.

Riesenberg judged that the project was at a critical stage, and that with further support and encouragement, a greater number of people would adopt a more positive attitude. In his opinion, the negative attitude expressed by most of the people was at least based partially on the assumption that the Americans would do more for Kili if they could be made to feel responsible and guilty for the Bikinians' unfortunate plight. He concluded:

> In other words, consciously or not, they are trying to place themselves in an advantageous bargaining position. An improvement in the general prosperity of Kili as a result of the development project may cause mitigation of this negativism. In any case, the project would seem to be a last chance for Kili, and is so viewed by some of the people; if it fails, they feel the only remaining recourse is to move elsewhere (Ibid.).

The district administration concurred that maximum effort should be made to support the project. To ensure that the people had an adequate food supply until they realized a harvest from their labor, local resources were supplemented by an issue of C-rations. In August the first of three special field trips was arranged to obtain more plantings from Kusaie. District anthropologist, Jack Tobin, accompanied Milne and a number of Bikinians on the trip. They returned to Kili with 6,000 taro cuttings and large quantities of breadfruit, banana, and other plants.

Tobin remained on Kili for several weeks. He observed that Milne and his team had earned the respect of most of the people and the majority were working under their guidance. It was reported that Milne continually encouraged the Bikinians about Kili's potential, and his own enthusiasm and optimism bolstered community morale and were converting a greater number of them to share a more positive view about their future. At the same time, the dissidents continued to lobby for additional aid. They admitted that conditions might improve in the future, but for the time being, they claimed they were poor and hungry, and they suggested that the Americans should do more in their behalf. At least two men refused to work in the swamp because they were not paid for their labor. Tobin attempted to persuade the dissidents that they were working for themselves and not for the government. They countered that they had not wished to relocate on Kili in the first place, and that in any event, the navy had promised to take care of them (Tobin 1954).

In late September the Bikinians divided the swamp among the *bamli* units. This division may have been necessitated by the unwillingness of some to join the communal effort. Initially, the *bamli* units continued to develop the swamp, and an agriculturalist who visited the island a short time later described the growth of the taro as amazing. In October the second voyage to Kusaie was made. Another 5,000 taro cuttings and other plants were returned to Kili.

Rapid progress in the development of a cooperative helped to alleviate some of the dissidents' influence. When the project began, the community's store had debts of several hundred dollars. Milne initiated an imaginative program in which Bikinians manufactured items for export. Using traditional skills, older men made wooden bowls and fathoms of coconut fiber sennit, and women produced articles of handicraft. The store purchased all copra and handicraft, and because the administration could not provide regular transportation, Milne made arrangements for a Marshallese trader to transport their goods. The sennit was sold to other Marshallese, and the handicraft found a ready market with Americans. One item in particular, a woman's purse of unique design created by Milne and dubbed the "Kili bag," soon became extremely popular and in demand by Americans throughout the entire Trust Territory and Guam. Profits from the copra

Plate 12. Bikinians drying copra on Kili Island, 1963. *(Photo by author.)*

Plate 13. Bikini woman preparing pandanus thatch panels for house roof on Kili Island, 1963. *(Photo by author.)*

and handicraft were substantial; within a year the store had assets of over $4,000. It was reorganized as the Kili Cooperative, in which every Bikinian held an equal share. It was hoped that in time the Cooperative would pay dividends, and even the most skeptical of the dissidents were pleased with the prospect.

As the project gained momentum the Bikinians requested materials to repair their dwellings. The houses were still structurally sound, but their tar-paper roofs had deteriorated since the founding of the settlement. As relatively few pandanus trees had been allowed on the former plantation and recent plantings had not yet matured, the supply of thatch was inadequate for the entire community. At the same time, however, some pandanus leaf that was available was left unused while the islanders requested assistance. It was evident that they had learned to appreciate that imports were more durable and required less time and effort than did the processing of thatch. Apparently in an effort to sustain the positive attitude that was developing in some quarters of the community, the administration eventually relented and provided corrugated metal roofing and a supply of nails.

The Project's Second Phase

In late 1955 Milne resigned his post. His replacement, Mr. Konto Sandbergen, was also an islander of mixed Micronesian-European ancestry. Like Milne, he had studied at the University of Hawaii and had taken work in community development and tropical agriculture. In October he joined Milne on Kili, and both men evaluated the project's progress. Milne's report indicated that over 23,000 taro plants were thriving and were well tended in the swamp. The number of breadfruit, papaya, pandanus, and banana trees had been greatly increased, and beds of sweet potatoes were doing well. Copra production for the year amounted to 90 tons, not far short of the 100 ton annual maximum achieved by the Japanese when Kili was a plantation (Milne 1955). Sandbergen's observations confirmed Milne's report, and both men travelled to Majuro for conferences with the administration.

Sandbergen returned to Kili in December. It was immediately apparent that the Kusaien, Milne's assistant, had not been able to provide the leadership required to sustain the project's momentum. The Bikinians had devoted little time to taro cultivation since October, and weeds were overtaking the swamp. In response to Sandbergen's urging, the council decided that each *bamli* was to spend one afternoon of each week working its section of the swamp. In late December the third and last trip was made to Kusaie to obtain an additional 5,000 taro cuttings and more breadfruit and banana plants. Planting the swamp was completed in January, 1956.

The Bikinians' lack of interest in taro cultivation, however, was becoming increasingly evident. Not enough time was being devoted to the crop each week to maintain it. Again in response to Sandbergen's urging, the council set aside a second afternoon of each week for work in the swamp. Some of the *bamli* responded; others did not. Most islanders simply did not like the arduous chore, and it is possible that they did not fully comprehend the benefits of sustained crop maintenance.

While Sandbergen was encountering some resistance on Kili, two or three members of the dissident group travelled to Majuro to register complaints with the district administrator. They claimed that more building materials were required for the repair of houses on Kili, and they were dissatisfied with the taro because the tubers were reportedly too small and took too long to grow. In early March one of those same Bikinians took advantage of a public meeting held at Majuro by the United Nations Visiting Mission to the Trust Territory. The Mission was composed of representatives from several nations and was accompanied by the High Commissioner. The meeting was a forum for any islander who wished to ask questions or raise issues about the administration of the Territory. The Bikinian informed the Mission that he and his fellows did not wish to remain on Kili. Further, he indicated that if they could not be returned to Bikini, they wished to be moved elsewhere. The High Commissioner responded that he was sympathetic to the Bikinians' position and told the Mission that the administration was in the process of providing the Bikinians with additional land at Jaluit. Further, attempts were being made to secure another vessel for the people's use and provide them with financial compensation for the loss of their homeland (Verbatim Account of Public Meeting; Marshallese People and U.N.

Visiting Mission, March 7, 1956). On the next day the High Commissioner took the Mission and the Bikinian to Jaluit by sea plane.
En route, the party flew over Kili to examine the island. A landing was made in Jaluit's lagoon, and the lands which were to be
set aside for the Bikinians were inspected. In its own report the
Mission noted that one of the main deterrents to Kili's development was the lack of regular transportation and that without a
vessel the Jaluit lands were of little value to the Bikinians. It concluded that " . . . every effort should be made to make shipping
available to the people of Kili without further delay" (U.N. Report on the Trust Territory of the Pacific Islands 1956:26-27).

Each of the welfare measures which the High Commissioner
reported upon had either been planned or under consideration
for some time. The possibility of providing the Bikinians with
land on Jaluit was first suggested as early as 1948 by the governor of the Marshalls when the Bikinians' selection of Kili was approved. Nothing came of the suggestion at the time, and anthropologist Drucker had recommended that the idea be reconsidered
when he reported upon his 1950 research on Kili. On one or two
occasions in the early 1950s, Juda and several of the Bikini *alab*
were taken to Jaluit to examine the lands under consideration.
The lands were 48.9 acres of former Japanese holdings which,
like Kili, had become public domain. They consisted of a parcel
known as Lojokar (24.5 acres) on the island of Jabwor in the
southeast sector of Jaluit and three small islands on the atoll's
northeast reef: Jebet (2.5 acres), Jar (3.4 acres), and Boklablab
(18.5 acres).

According to the administration's plan, the Bikinians were
to establish a colony on Lojokar and develop it and the three islands to supplement the community's copra and subsistence base.
It was projected that the colony site would provide a safe anchorage for a vessel which could service Kili as had been done in Japanese times. It was also hoped that fish caught in Jaluit's lagoon
and in the open sea between Jaluit and Kili would compensate
for Kili's meager marine resources.

The plan was beset with complications from the beginning.
One boundary of Lojokar was not clearly defined. For a time
there was some confusion as to whether or not Boklablab was in
the public domain because some Jaluit people claimed it as their

own. The claim was judged invalid by the administration, but the dispute and the vagueness of Lojokar's boundary made the Bikinians insecure about their right to the land, and they feared that a colony there would result in conflict with the Jaluit people. Further, the Bikinians judged the Jaluit lands to be too rocky and therefore of little value; they also resisted the idea of dividing their community for the purpose of forming a colony.

Regardless of the Bikinians' reservations, the administration had laid concrete plans for the colony during the initial phase of the Kili project. By the end of May, 1955 a half dozen dwellings and two warehouses had been constructed on Lojokar. To provide direct communication with Majuro, radio receivers and transmitters, generators, and fuel storage facilities had been installed on Kili and Lojokar. During the remainder of the year the administration had encouraged the Bikinians to send colonists to Jaluit. For a number of reasons the people failed to respond. A vessel had yet to be provided; the Bikinians had no legal status with regard to the Jaluit lands; and they still feared the reaction of the Jaluit people. The Bikinians also argued that Lojokar had almost no subsistence crops and that colonists could not possibly support themselves without aid.

The absence of dependable shipping not only impeded any progress on the colony, it also curtailed the lucrative export business the Bikinians had established. The private trading arrangements made by Milne had ended with his resignation. The popular Kili bags were purchased by administration officials on the field trip vessels and were channelled to markets, but other handicraft items ceased to be produced. To solve the transportation problem, the High Commissioner created a special fund, and the administration in the Marshalls considered several locally available vessels. In September, 1955, the *Ijuran* 'Morning Star', a fifty-four-foot vessel owned by the Protestant mission, was purchased for the project. It had a cargo capacity of twenty tons and was powered by both sail and diesel engine.

The *Ijuran* was badly in need of overhaul, and repairs were not completed until May or June of 1956. The vessel was rechristened the *Libra* and was placed under Sandbergen's supervision with the stipulation that it was only to be used for the Kili project. A captain and an engineer, both Marshallese, were hired to train the Bikinians to operate the ship. The Bikinians were to receive title to the *Libra* when they had acquired the skills necessary for operating it.

It soon became apparent that not all aspects of the *Libra*'s operation had been foreseen. The administration in the Marshalls notified the High Commissioner that $8,500 was required for annual costs of the crew's salary and subsistence, normal ship maintenance, and fuel. It had not been considered that the vessel could not be self-supporting. The High Commissioner accepted the necessity of employing a captain and engineer, but he questioned the desirability of paying Bikinians to man their own vessel. The administration in the Marshalls agreed that as temporary measures salaries and subsistence for the crew were unfortunate but practical necessities. Since the Libra could not remain off Kili and had to be stationed at Jaluit, crewmen could not subsist themselves just as colonists could not.

The Territory administration was thus in the embarrassing position of having acquired a vessel for the Bikinians which they could not afford, and the High Commissioner had little alternative but to allot funds in order to honor his pledge to the islanders and to the United Nations. With reluctance, he made arrangements to provide wages for the crew and subsistence for both crewmen and the Jaluit colonists. Late in the summer of 1954 Sandbergen moved to Jabwor to get the colony underway. One or two married crewman on the *Libra* moved their nuclear families to Lojokar, but the Bikinians were still reluctant to send colonists.

Some change in the Bikinians' attitude occurred by October, 1956 when the Americans renewed negotiations pertaining to the legal disposition of Kili, the Jaluit lands, and Bikini, and they began to discuss plans for providing the Bikinians with financial compensation. The administration was anxious to have the issue resolved since the United States had never received more than the islanders' verbal consent to use Bikini. In accord with the Bikinians' wishes, it was proposed that separate agreements be made with the paramount chief and with themselves. By that date the former paramount chief had been succeeded by his heir; the latter and his own heirs apparent were offered $15,000 for whatever claims they had to Bikini. In exchange for indefinite use of

Bikini, the Bikinians were offered indefinite use of Kili and the Jaluit lands, a one-time lump sum payment of $25,000, and a trust fund of $300,000 yielding semi-annual interest payments of $4,972.50.

With Juda and the Jitoen headman as their principal spokesmen, the Bikinians responded with unanimity on two issues. First, they reaffirmed that they would not agree to any settlement which included the paramount chief. Secondly, they had learned from experience and did not trust verbal promises; they demanded that all facets of the settlement be committed to paper. When it was made clear that the administration's proposal was in accord with their demands, the Bikinians indicated their willingness to accept it. Remarks made at the conclusion of a meeting with officials clearly revealed that the Bikinians wanted the United States to assume the responsibility for their welfare. The Jitoen headman noted:

> We are on this island; it is much too small; there are many people, but never mind, we are waiting for you to make things better for us (Letter to High Commissioner from J. Tobin, District Anthropologist, October 17, 1956).

Juda reiterated:

> ... the responsibility is the Government's. We are putting it into your hands; we are willing to go as you say (Ibid.).

With basic negotiations completed, the High Commissioner arrived at Kili in early November to finalize the agreement. He informed the people that:

> I was in Bikini this past April, flew over Bikini, rode in the lagoon and walked over the land, and it will be many years before you can go back, it will be a long, a very long time.

> The United States Government does not want to own Bikini and to forever have the title, only use it so long as they may need it for the most good for all the people of the world . . . .

> Because I know it is a long time before you can go back to Bikini I want the Trust Territory Government to be good to you and I want you to know what we want to do for you.

To repeat, in addition to giving you the right to use Kili, as the government wants to use Bikini, we have given you Jebet, Jar, Boklablab,
part of Jabwor, the boat and are helping you with agriculture problems
on Kili (Verbatim account of High Commissioner's Meeting with Bikini
people, prepared by Marshalls District Anthropologist; November 10,
1956).

The terms of the proposed agreement were reviewed, and the
High Commissioner responded to questions. The Bikinians wanted to be certain that by accepting this agreement they were not
eliminating the possibility of further government assistance, and
Juda asked that if the people experienced future difficulties would
they be able to ask for help. The High Commissioner replied that
they would be treated the same as other Marshallese in the advent
of typhoon damage or other serious perils. In response to other
questions, he explained that if the United States needed to use
Bikini forever, they would receive no additional compensation.
On the other hand, if and when it was possible for them to return
to Bikini, he assured them they would not have to return any of
the money. It was theirs forever.
    When the High Commissioner was assured that the Bikinians
understood and were satisfied, he told them that the $25,000 pay-
ment would soon be delivered and they would be asked to sign
the agreement. Later in the month, the paramount chief and his
heirs were approached with the proposal to award them $15,000
in exchange for their rights to Bikini. They refused the offer, and
a settlement was never reached.
    On November 26, an official delivered the $25,000 and ob-
tained the signatures of the Bikini *alab* on copies of the agreement
which were prepared in both English and Marshallese. Two items
in the negotiations and agreement are worthy of special note.
First, neither the High Commissioner nor the agreement ruled out
the possibility that the Bikinians might someday be returned to
Bikini. While it was stressed that such an event could only be in
the far distant future, it was important that the option was left
open. Secondly, the agreement did not give the Bikinians a title
of ownership to Kili and the Jaluit lands. This point of the agreement clearly states that the Bikinians acquired only full use rights
to Kili and the Jaluit lands until such time as they are returned
to Bikini (see Appendix).

The Bikinians reacted with great enthusiasm to the bonanza represented by the lump sum payment. They viewed it and the trust fund as payment for their loss of Bikini land, and as a consequence, they decided that every individual who had land rights to the atoll were entitled to shares. Three categories of people were distinguished for the division of the $25,000. Each of those resident on Kili received $79; people who were temporarily away were allotted $75 each; and those living elsewhere on a permanent basis were allotted $50 each.

Several consequences of the $25,000 payment were immediate. There was a run on the Cooperative which was depleted of stores. Some people took trips to Majuro and Kwajalein to see relatives and purchase trade goods. The two major trading companies in the Marshalls sent large quantities of goods on the next field trip vessel. Representatives of both arrived to sell stock, and a few Bikinians invested some of their new riches.

The trust fund was established in late 1956 with semi-annual interest payments due on the first day of January and July. The first interest payment was delivered to Kili on July 4, 1957. A policy was implemented allotting one amount to people resident on the island and a smaller share to those living elsewhere. In July, 1954 each person on Kili received a share of $16.75, and every islander who had land rights at Bikini but was not resident on the island was allotted $10.25.

The land settlement, financial compensation, the *Libra,* and the guarantee of subsistence for colonists all served to create a mood of optimism in the community and made the Bikinians more secure about their right to occupy the Jaluit lands. Shortly after the initial negotiations on Kili in October, 1956, a list of volunteer colonists was compiled. In order to ensure that not all able-bodied members of the same *bamli* would leave and neglect their land on Kili, the council made the final selection. Generally, only one nuclear family was selected from any one *bamli* at any given time. By late 1956 three families were living at Jaluit as colonists, and in early 1957 a fourth was added. During the year, another three or four families alternated with the original set. As one family returned to Kili on the *Libra,* another travelled to Jaluit as a replacement. Not counting the crewmen and their dependents, the number of colonists varied from twenty to twenty-five individuals at any one time. A branch of the Kili Cooperative was established at the colony, and its warehouses served to store copra lifted from Kili.

Initially, the work on Jaluit went well. Regular radio contact with Kili was maintained; the *Libra* shuttled back and forth between the home island, and occasional trips were made to Majuro. Under Sandbergen's direction, the colonists cleared land and began planting. Life on Jabwor was more varied than on Kili. In the 1950s Jabwor had partly regained its pre-war position as an important center of trade and other activities. Both of the major trading companies had branches on the island, and the Protestant and Catholic missions had schools there. An experimental agricultural station manned by an American was located near Lojokar. People from all over Jaluit visited Jabwor, and some awaited the arrival of field trip vessels there.

Despite their fears, the Bikinians had considerable contact with the Jaluit people. They attended church services at the Protestant mission, and a few developed personal friendships with local islanders. Some Jaluit people visited the Bikinians and made purchases from the branch of the Kili Cooperative. For the most part, relations between the Bikinians and the Jaluit people were cordial, but the imprecise boundary of Lojokar remained a source of concern, and colonists refused to work or plant near the area. A few Jaluit people told the Bikinians that Lojokar had never been Japanese property and should not have been made available to them. Further, the islanders who had laid claim earlier to Boklablab raised the issue again by charging that the island had been illegally seized by the Japanese and had thus never been at the disposal of the Americans. Because of the tensions over land, the Bikinians were never completely at ease with at least some of the people of Jaluit.

Regardless of the uncertainties over land, Sandbergen kept the colonists hard at work. By October, 1957 most of Lojokar had been cleared and a number of coconut and pandanus trees had been planted. No work had yet been done on the three islands, but plans were made to develop Boklablab (Tobin 1957).

In the latter part of 1957 some Bikinians were beginning to emerge from their self-imposed isolation. While many were still hesitant to seek contacts outside their own circle, some had acquired a broader view of their island world from their experiences with outsiders since their initial relocation. Those who travelled aboard the *Libra,* served as colonists, or ventured to Majuro and/ or Kwajalein gained further sophistication about the ways of other islanders. It was reported that some Bikinians were developing a more positive view of themselves and were beginning to identify with and be more confident in their interactions with other Marshallese (Mason 1958).

The change in the Bikinians' self-image and the over-all progress of the project were quite encouraging. For the first time it appeared that they might make a satisfactory adjustment to their new home. The *Libra*'s operation considerably brightened the people's prospects. The vessel was able to service Kili during the beginning of the period of rough seas in late 1957. With the aid of the radio communication system advantage could be taken of occasional calms, and the *Libra* made the quick run to Kili, picked up copra and passengers, and unloaded food and other cargo.

On the other hand, the withdrawal of supervisory personnel on Kili had some undesirable consequences. When the work of the taro and handicraft specialists was completed their employment ended. With Sandbergen stationed at the colony, the Bikinians had become even more lax in their care of the taro swamp which was being overtaken by weeds. Copra and handicraft production had fallen off markedly. The $25,000 and the initial interest payments had provided the people with a greater income than they had ever had, and they had little incentive to prepare copra or handicraft. Recently planted breadfruit, pandanus, and bananas were doing well, however, and there had been a definite net gain in the quantity of subsistence crops.

Typhoon Disaster

The project suffered irreversible setbacks in late 1957. In early November the *Libra* was caught off Kili in the fury of typhoon Lola. No loss of life was incurred, but the vessel sank with several hundred dollars of cargo. Seawater was washed into the taro swamp. Breadfruit trees were stripped bare, large numbers of palms were downed, and other crops were damaged. In early January, 1958 typhoon Ophelia caused even greater destruction on Jaluit and other southern atolls. The Jaluit colony was devastated. None of the colonists was harmed, and they were all returned to Kili. The destruction caused by the typhoons brought an end to almost all that had been accomplished. A survey of Kili revealed that copra and food resources would be drastically reduced for months. The Cooperative's resources were being rapidly depleted, and the administration had no alternative but to provide relief foods.

After the typhoons, the Bikinians were little better off than they had been during the initial years of the resettlement. Even with the damage, the quantity of subsistence crops was somewhat greater than when the people had first arrived, but this gain was offset by an increase in the size of the community. The modest medical program initiated in the mid-1940s had continued to have unanticipated effects. The reduced infant mortality rate and general improvement in the people's health had swelled the community to over 240 individuals. To worsen their prospects, the rehabilitation of Jaluit and other typhoon-struck atolls required most of the administration's attention, and Sandbergen was assigned elsewhere. It was hoped that the Bikinians would employ the skills they had learned to rehabilitate Kili with little outside supervision, but such hope was unwarranted. The emergency foods were soon exhausted, and in mid-1958, the Bikinians were placed on a food relief program. At three-month intervals over the next year and a half, they were provided with substantial quantities of rice and flour.

In the spring of 1959 another vessel, the *Libra II,* was acquired. It had been constructed in Hong Kong upon special order from the Trust Territory for the Bikinians. As before a captain and an engineer were hired, and the Bikinians served as deckhands. In reality the *Libra II* proved to be of little use to the people. Because of the need for transportation among the typhoon damaged atolls, it was used for their rehabilitation and was scheduled to call at Kili only every third month. Further, numerous difficulties were experienced with the craft. It was poorly designed and proved to be top heavy and unstable. It was frequently at Majuro for repair.

Both the *Libra II* and regular field trip vessels were not able to provide adequate service throughout 1960. Food shortages again occurred, and the year ended like many of the previous ones. A ship called at Kili in December:

> No council meeting, the field trip officer was afraid to go ashore. The sea was quite rough . . . discharged $460 worth of trade goods. No copra loaded, bad loading conditions (Marshalls District Field Trip Report, December 16, 1960).

Problems with the *Libra II* continued, and it was eventually beached at Majuro in a state of total disrepair. The vessel was declared unsightly debris and was dismantled (Kiste 1968:366-367).

Two years after the typhoon most of the damaged trees on Kili had recovered. A few people planted more breadfruit, but most planted the coconut and pandanus trees with which they had always been familiar. Some effort was being made to keep the groves free from brush, but planting techniques introduced by the project were not employed. The saline content of the swamp was dissipated, but no effort was made to replant taro; the swamp lay abandoned.

The winter seasons were made more difficult than they otherwise might have been due to the lack of agricultural activity, and on more than one occasion the islanders were again reduced to a diet of immature coconuts. Their earlier conviction that Kili was not habitable was reaffirmed. They had realized no lasting return from the efforts which had been expended during the development project, and they were unwilling to commit themselves to such an effort again without assistance.

The Early 1960s

In 1961 the administration once again considered relocating the community, and the issue was discussed with the people. The Bikinians affirmed that they would like to move again, and on one occasion, Juda gave an impassioned speech which clearly revealed the stance that they had developed over the years.[1]

---

[1] Juda made two factual errors in his speech. In 1961, the Bikinians had been on Kili for almost thirteen years, and not ten. Further, Juda was ap-

I would like to give you some history of Kili Island. We were moved here by the government 10 years ago. It was not the place we wanted to go to but the government decided that we should live here. In all these years we have tried to live here but there are many things that have come up which make it very difficult for us to make a living here. Today is a good example of what has happened in the past 10 years, it is too rough to work copra, so we are unable to sell our copra and buy food. It doesn't matter how long a ship waits off of Kili, if it is rough it is rough and we cannot get our copra to the ship or bring in food. Our group of people here is getting larger every year and is increasing every year. It is difficult to take care of these people and the island is too small for them to live on. In a little while there will not be enough copra on the island to feed all the people.

The relocation of the Kili people is up to the government. We would like to return to Bikini, which is our home but realize that we cannot do this as the Atomic Energy Commission is using it for exploding of bombs. We also know that Bikini plays a big part in World affairs and we realize this importance. The Government moved us and not our paramount chief. If the chief had moved us then it would be up to the chief to find another place for us. We want to move to government land only and will not move to lands owned by the chief.

Bikini is larger than Kili and we had plenty of land and a big lagoon. The Government moved us, therefore, it is up to the Government to find us a new place which is larger than Kili and better for the people.

Now the Government knows our condition, it is, therefore, up to the Government to find us a place (Memorandum to Distad Marshalls from Assistant Distad Marshalls, April 16, 1961).

The possibility of another relocation was considered in the offices of the High Commissioner. Official correspondence at the time revealed that the administration was beginning to abandon all hope of making the Kili resettlement a success. No action was taken, however, and within a short time, attempts were made again to convince the Bikinians that they had no alternative but to remain on Kili. Those *alab* who had led the dissident faction earlier emerged now as vocal critics of the Americans and as forces potent in influencing public opinion.

The islanders still harbored the hope of returning to Bikini. Memories of the atoll had become increasingly distorted with

---

parently under the impression that nuclear tests were still being conducted at Bikini, whereas the last test had occurred in 1957.

time. In the accounts of elders, life at Bikini had become a Golden Age, and young Bikinians came to believe that no one had ever suffered want or discomfort there. When urged to improve their lot on Kili, the Bikinians responded that the Americans had caused their relocation and were responsible for their future. A number of islanders frequently travelled to the district center to appeal for more aid and request that they be returned to Bikini or moved elsewhere. They often asked (without success) that the administration subsist and house them while they were at Majuro, and their appearances there became so frequent that Americans referred to them as the "usual Kili recreation."

When surf conditions allowed cargo to be unloaded at Kili, the semi-annual interest payments from the trust fund enabled the Bikinians to supplement the island's subsistence resources. The payments continued to have other consequences as well. A sizeable amount of cash was expended for material items. The people acquired a greater quantity of those trade goods which they had always purchased, and ready-to-wear clothing became more common. Some people bought small camp-style kerosene stoves, transistor radios and other novel items. The payments continued to have a negative effect on copra production. Even in the calm summer months, the people produced little or no copra in the weeks prior to the July payment. The money was much greater than income derived from a few weeks of copra production and allowed the people to care for their immediate needs. In the long run, the Bikinians lost income as nuts deteriorated on the ground.

The Bikinians' desire for imported goods had also increased with their new purchasing power, and during the early 1960s they began to make requests to draw large sums from the trust fund's principal or to have it increased. Other Marshallese told Bikinians that they had been unwise and should have held out for a larger sum. Financial settlements paid to other islanders caused the Bikinians to reevaluate their trust fund. In 1964 the people of Kwajalein received $750,000 for a ninety-nine year lease on some of the land occupied by the military on the atoll. Over $900,000 was paid to the people of Rongelab Atoll as compensation for injuries and discomforts caused by radioactive fallout from one of the tests conducted at Bikini in 1954 (see Hines

1962:157-195). Both settlements were one-time payments which
did not provide a perpetual income, but the Bikinians were only
impressed with the amounts, and they felt that they had suffered
another injustice.

The continued expansion of the population on Kili reduced
the size of individual shares from the interest payments and made
it increasingly difficult for the Bikinians to achieve a minimum
subsistence level during the winter seasons. By the time of my
first fieldwork in 1963-64, the community had grown to over 280
individuals (see Table 3.1). As in earlier years, some people occasionally returned to Kwajalein to find relief from Kili and supplement their cash income. A few individuals found employment
with government agencies at Majuro, and others travelled there
for medical purposes as well as respite from Kili.

By the 1960s Kwajalein had become an important site in the
United States's ballistic missile testing program. Islanders there
witnessed the launching of missiles which intercepted interconti-
nental missiles fired from the west coast of the United States. Bikinians who remained at home learned of the American rocket
and space program from those who travelled to Kwajalein and
from radio broadcasts. Satellites orbiting the earth are quite visible in the clear night sky of the Pacific, and having heard of manned space flights, the Bikinians assumed that all the satellites
were spacecraft piloted by Americans.

American missile and space technology was further evidence
of the capabilities of the United States and reaffirmed the Bikinians' belief that it would be but a small matter for the Americans
to remedy their plight on Kili. On numerous occasions they re-
counted the problems posed by Kili's reef, the increasing pressure
of the population on the small island, and the hardships they had
endured. The wealth and technological know-how of the United
States and the Americans' obligation to them were frequently
mentioned. One evening I sat with a group of people on Kili's
beach and watched a satellite cut its glowing path against the sky.
One old man asked:

> Why is it you Americans are so smart and powerful that you can send
> men to the moon, but you can't help us with our problems here on
> Kili?

The islanders' stance of dependence that had developed over the years was manifest in other ways and was reinforced, albeit unwittingly, by the administration. A school lunch program modeled after those in the United States was initiated for students in the Marshall Islands. The administration assumed that foodstuffs could be delivered to communities and that their consumption would be limited to school children. Accordingly, in the fall of 1963 several hundred pounds of United States Department of Agriculture (USDA) surplus rice, flour, and other commodities were unloaded at Kili. For a time adult volunteers prepared a noon meal for students each school day. This changed in November with the usual winter seas and the beginning of the lean season. By December the council began distributing the USDA food among the households. Supplies were exhausted when a calm spell coincided with the arrival of a field trip ship. More food and other cargo were brought ashore. With the second supply of USDA largesse on hand, people purchased little food with their own cash. Within a short time the surplus commodities were again being distributed. These supplies prevented the annual food shortage from reaching critical proportions, and from the Bikinians' point of view, the wealth of the United States had once again been demonstrated.[2]

By the early sixties dwellings were again in great need of repair. The metal roofing provided a decade earlier had largely rusted away, and the original wooden floors and walls had deteriorated badly. Contrary to their wishes but out of necessity, many of the islanders had reroofed their dwellings with thatch. Requests were made for building materials, but the administration encouraged the people to use their interest payments to buy what they needed. The Bikinians rejected the suggestion; from their point of view, the income was compensation for their loss of Bikini, and it was unfair to pressure them to use it for the necessities of life on Kili. Further, they argued that it was the Americans' responsibility to ensure that housing on Kili was adequate because they had moved them there. The earlier charge that the

---

[2] The USDA school lunch program has had similar results in other Marshallese communities. Islanders on a number of atolls now consider the surplus foods as a regular subsistence source, and the program has generally had an adverse effect on agricultural production.

votes in the 1948 plebiscite had been miscounted had now been transformed: some individuals contended that the Americans had deliberately rigged the entire affair.

Summary and Analysis

The Kili Development Project had few of the consequences that the Americans had intended. The Bikinians committed themselves to developing Kili's agricultural potential only when they had little hope of another relocation and when their efforts were guided by outside supervision. What had been accomplished during the project was negated by damage and discouragement from natural disasters, the withdrawal of supervisory personnel, and the islanders' continuing desire to return to Bikini or to be resettled elsewhere.

The administration initiated the project as an attempt to help the people achieve a satisfactory adjustment to their new home and to end problems that had resulted from their relocations. At the same time it is clear that during the latter part of the project, the administration was responding to the threat of embarrassment and pressure exerted by the United Nations Trusteeship Council. The administration had little alternative but to mobilize the effort required for the fulfillment of commitments made to the United Nations. The American effort to assist the Bikinians was thus largely a consequence of external forces as it was in the earlier period at Rongerik.

The Kili Development Project also reinforced the Bikinians' notion that the United States should assume the responsibility for their welfare and had the resources to do so. The provision of manpower and other resources required by the project (vessels, radio equipment, housing at Jaluit, etc.) served as further demonstration of what the Americans could do when they desired. Other welfare measures implemented after the project's termination, the Bikinians' experiences at Kwajalein, and their awareness of the United States missile and space technology represented still more dramatic evidence of the magnitude of American power and resources, and reaffirmed the Bikinians' earlier conclusion that it was to their advantage to attach themselves firmly to the Americans.

From the Bikinians' point of view, one major goal was achieved during the project. To them, the agreement with the United States represented an end to their subordinate status vis-a-vis the paramount chief. As he had no legal or traditional claim to Kili, he had no right to their services or resources, and in their eyes, a significant victory had been won.

The financial compensation awarded the islanders increased their ability to purchase imported foods and material items. This in turn increased the people's desire for a wider range of goods, a process that had begun early in their relocations, and made them more dependent upon the Americans and the outside world. At the same time, the Bikinians' income gave them less incentive to engage in the production of copra and handicraft as a means of satisfying their wants.

By the later 1950s and early 1960s, the experience that the people had acquired since their initial relocation and the corresponding improvement in their own self-image gave them a greater confidence in themselves. These changes in the people's attitudes were manifest in their assertiveness in making numerous petitions to the administration and the strong stance taken by Juda and others in dealings with Americans. The Bikinians were no longer the meek and uncertain islanders who had readily acquiesced to the Americans' request for their relocation a decade and a half earlier.

CHAPTER SEVEN

Consequences
of the Land Division

By the 1960s the pressures of the expanding population on Kili had heightened the Bikinians' concern over the small size of their landholdings. In 1964 there were 282 individuals resident on the island, an increase of 112 people (or sixty percent) over the pre-relocation community at Bikini (see Tables 3.1 and 3.2, pages 39 and 40).

A substantial increase in the number of individuals living elsewhere who could claim rights to the community's land further contributed to the islanders' anxiety over land. Expatriates on other atolls had continued to have children, and as the latter married and had offspring of their own, the number of people with potential rights to Kili land had expanded. Marriage with outsiders had also become more frequent, reflecting the Bikinians' increased willingness to interact with other Marshallese and the more positive reputation they had gained with them. More marriages outside the community, however, did not result in a significant growth in the number of non-Bikinians who were actually resident on Kili. Kili was no more attractive to other islanders than it was to Bikinians, and eight of forty-four married couples on the island (18.1 percent) represented unions with outsiders, only a slight increase over the 13.7 percent of such unions in the pre-relocation community. The number of islanders belonging to the three main Bikini sub-clans who were residing elsewhere and had acquired spouses from other atolls, however, had grown from the nine of pre-relocation times to twenty-four (see Table 3.6, page 50). By 1964 absentee clansmen, the children of absentee male clansmen, and spouses from other communities totalled 177 (see Tables 3.3 and 3.4, pages 41 and 42).

The increasing population on Kili and the growing number of kinsmen elsewhere, helped evoke memories of Bikini's twenty-six islands, and the people recalled the time when they had rights to a number of land parcels and not just a single plot. The Bikini *alab* were the most outspoken in their discontent. Some claimed that they had not received an equitable share in the land division, and others regretted ever having agreed to Juda's scheme. The Kili *alab* shared in the general discontent over the small land parcels, but they were pleased with their recently acquired status. As one of them expressed it:

> Here I have *kajur* 'power'. At Bikini only the old *alab* had power, but now I have some land here and have power.

The New Scheme of Land Tenure

Regardless of their satisfactions and dissatisfactions with the *bamli* landholding scheme, the islanders became aware in the years immediately after the land division, that they had not foreseen its ramifications and were attempting to cope with its inherent problems. Land had always been held by groups of unilineally aligned kinsmen, that is, by members of a matrilineage or members of a patri-centered corporation composed of a male and his own children. *Alab* rights had always been inherited within the framework of one or the other of these two sets of relatives. Members of either type of corporation had always possessed worker rights to its land which were conceptually distinct from the usufruct rights extended to others (affines, adopted children, and in the case of matrilineages, the children of males).

Residence in 1954 had determined to a large extent the membership of the *bamli* units. Like the households from which they were derived, the *bamli* units were neither structured around the lineages nor any other single organizational principle. Various combinations of matrilineal, agnatic, and affinal kinsmen comprised the units, and with the exception of the *alab*, the rights of *bamli* members were not differentiated. Aside from the *alab*, ev-

ery *bamli* member held equal right to its land, and at the time of
the land division, no thought was given as to how land rights
were to be determined in the future. Thus, the Bikinians had
created a situation where the traditional cultural norms which
governed the transmission of land rights over time were no longer congruent with the actual social structure of their landholding
corporations.[1]

The composition of the *bamli* units was recorded in 1957
and 1964, and the data are tabulated in Tables 7.1 and 7.2. Indicated in parentheses are islanders included as *bamli* members
but who had been absent from the community since Japanese
times or who had never participated in the resettlements. As of
1957, no individual belonged to more than one *bamli*, and each
corporation was a discrete unit. The total membership of the
nineteen *bamli* in 1957 was 336.

The problems inherent in the *bamli* landholding scheme
were essentially two-fold. First, it was necessary for the Bikinians to determine how *alab* rights were to be inherited and how
males would succeed to the headship of the *bamli* units. Secondly, there was the problem of determining how *bamli* memberships
were to be defined when marriages and births occurred. More
specifically, the islanders were uncertain whether individuals who
married after the land division were to become members of their
spouse's *bamli* or were to have some right to one another's land.
Children born to couples married after the division posed a similar problem. Were they to be included as members of their father's *bamli* or their mother's—or both? In examining the problems presented by the *bamli* organization, it is useful to divide
the nineteen units into two types on the basis of their composition as of 1957.

Type-One Bamli. None of these thirteen *bamli* included the
headman's sisters or sisters' children; see Table 7.1. With two exceptions, the core of each was either a nuclear or cognatic extended family including both sons and daughters of the *alab*. In several instances, one or more other relatives of the core family were

---

[1] Geertz (1957) has provided a useful discussion of the theoretical implica-
tions of situations where incongruities have developed between the cultural
norms and expectations and the actual social organization of a society.

Table 7.1. Type-one Landholding *Bamli*

Bamli	1		2		3		6		7		12	
Year	1957	1964	1957	1964	1957	1964	1957	1964	1957	1964	1957	1964
Alab	o	o	B	B	N	N's so	T	T	a	a	q	q
Alab (1957)	1	1	1	1	1		1	1	1	1	1	1
Alab's wi	1	1	1	1	1	1	1	1	1	1		(1)
Alab's wi so		1										
Alab's mo											(1)	(1)
Alab's gr mo											(1)	
Alab's so		1	5	5	3	3	7	7	3	3	1	1
Alab's so wi			2	2		3		2	1	1		
Alab's adopted so					1	1						
Alab's adopted so wi												
Alab's da	2	4	2	2	4	3	2	2	5	7		
Alab's da hu	1	1	1	2					3	3		
Alab's adopted da			2	2								
Alab's adopted da hu				1								
Alab's gr ch	6	12	11	22	4	13	2	6	10	27		
Alab's gr gr ch		1										
Alab's br							1	1				
Alab's br wi												
Alab's so wi mo												
Alab's so wi si			1									
Alab's so wi si ch												
Alab's da hu si												
Alab's da hu si ch												
Other												1(2)
Totals 1957	11		26		14		14		24		4	
Totals 1964		22		38		24		20		43		7

included as *bamli* members. In two cases, numbers 6 and 19, the headman's younger brother was a *bamli* member. In eleven of the thirteen, all of the headman's children were *bamli* members; a twelfth, number 3, lacked only one of the head's four sons.

One of the two exceptional units was number 1. It includ-

13		14		15		16		17		18		19	
1957	1964	1957	1964	1957	1964	1957	1964	1957	1964	1957	1964	1957	1964
c	*c*	Juda	Juda	*u*	*u*	*d*	*d*	*A*	*A*'s so[a]	*p*	*p*	*b*	*b*
1	1	1	1	1	1	1	1	1		1	1	1	1
1		1		1	1		1	1	1			1	1
1	1	4	3	3	3	2	2			3	3		
		2	3	1	2	2	2				2		
3	2							1	2			2	2
	1												
3	3	4	4	5	6	6	4					1	1
		2	3	1	4	2	3						
1	7	17	29	12	21	12	26			1	3		1
			1										
										(1)	(1)		
										(1)			
		1	1			1	1						
		1	1										
			1										
		2	2										
		2	4										
10		37		24		26		3		5		7	
	15		53		38		40		3		9		7

[a] Adopted sons.

ed the headman's unmarried daughter, married daughter and the latter's husband and children, but it did not include his only son. The second, number 12, was the *bamli* composed of the members of the small Makaoliej lineage segment M 3/3 and the son of its only male.

Table 7.2. Type-two Landholding *Bamli*

Bamli	4		5		8		9		10		11	
Year	1957	1964	1957	1964	1957	1964	1957	1964	1957	1964	1957	1964
Alab	R	R	S's so	S's so	C	C	M	M	Lok-wiar's so	Lok-wiar's so	L	L's so
Alab (1957)	1	1	1	1	1	1	1	1	1	1	1	
Alab's wi	1	1	1	1	1	1			1	1	1	1
Alab's wi da											1	1
Alab's mo			1	1								
Alab's so	3	3	2	2					1	1	3(1)	3(1)
Alab's so wi	1	1	1								(1)[a]	1(1)[a]
Alab's adopted so						2						
Alab's da	1	1	3	3	1	1			3	2	1	1
Alab's da hu	1[b]	1[b]		2		1						1
Alab's adopted da	2	2				2						
Alab's gr ch	7	13	2	6	1	5			2	5	5(9)	9(9)
Alab's gr gr ch		1										(4)
Alab's br			1	1					(1)	(1)		
Alab's br wi			1	1					(1)	(1)		
Alab's br so			3	2			1	1	(3)	(4)		
Alab's br so wi								1	(2)	(4)		
Alab's br da			5	8								
Alab's br gr ch				2								
Alab's si			2	2			2	2	3(1)	3(1)		
Alab's si hu			1	2			2	2	2(1)	1(1)		
Alab's si so	b	b	1	2	(1)		3	3	1	1	(2)	
Alab's si so wi					(1)						(2)	
Alab's si da				3	1	1	1	2		2	a	a
Alab's si da hu					1	1						
Alab's si da hu br					1							
Alab's si gr ch					3(3)	3						(10)
Alab's si gr gr ch					4	7						
Other					1	1						
Totals 1957	17		24		20		10		23		37	
Totals 1964		24		40		26		12		29		32

[a] *L*'s so wi is also *L*'s si da.   [b] *R*'s da hu is also *R*'s si so.

Type-Two Bamli. The remaining six *bamli* varied in the particulars of organization but, with one exception, all included the
head's own children and his sister's children, who had always
been rivals in the competition over land rights. Consequently,
the composition of these units posed exceedingly difficult problems for determining the future disposition of *alab* rights.

Two of these units, numbers 5 and 10, were headed by the
eldest sons of the two Bikini *alab* (Lokwiar and *alab S*) who had
died prior to the land division without matrilineal heirs. The
households from which the two *bamli* were derived had been cognatic extended families that upon the deaths of the two old *alab*
had been transformed into joint sibling families. From the stand-
point of the eldest sons who had succeeded their fathers, their
bamli units included numerous kinsmen who could be expected
to advance claims to be their rightful heirs and successors. In
each of the two cases, the headman's brothers and sisters' sons
as well as his own sons were members of the *bamli.*

Three of the type-two units, numbers 4, 8, and 11, counted
among their members all or most of the headman's own children,
some of his sister's sons and daughters, and offspring of the latter.
In one of the three, number 11 headed by *alab L,* all of the headman's sister's children were among the group of expatriates who
had established themselves on Ailinglablab in Japanese times.

The remaining *bamli* number 9 was unique. It was headed
by the only unmarried *alab* and included his sisters, their husbands and children, and the son of his deceased brother.

Thus, with the exception of *bamli* 9, type-two units included the head's own children and sisters' children who, in the traditional system of land tenure, had never belonged to the same
landholding group. With the new order on Kili, they shared common membership in the same corporation—a situation rich in its
potential for conflict.

Alab Rights. As the Bikinians became aware of the problems
inherent in the *bamli* scheme, council meetings were frequently
devoted to discussing possible solutions. The range of alternatives
considered, however, was restricted by conceptions rooted in the
former system of inheritance and succession. In the past, a headman's potential heirs were limited to three categories of kinsmen:
younger brother, maternal nephew, and under conditions which

have been specified, his own son. Discussions on Kili focused upon these three categories of kinsmen and which one would be designated as heir and successor of headmen within the framework of
the *bamli* units. Such other males as affinal kin of the headman
belonging to the *bamli* were never considered as potential heirs to
the *alab*.

Members of the two types of *bamli* were confronted with
somewhat different problems as they attempted to make some
decision about the future disposition of *alab* rights. Islanders belonging to type-one *bamli* were uncertain as to whether or not the
heirs and successors to their respective *alab* would be chosen from
within their own *bamli* units. While none of the type-one *bamli*
included maternal nephews of the *alab*, seven of the thirteen headmen did have sisters' sons who belonged to, and in some instances
headed, other *bamli*. Further, three of the thirteen had younger
brothers who headed other *bamli*. In the new order on Kili, the
status of the headmen's nephews and brothers who were members
of other *bamli* was unclear, and it was also uncertain as to whether or not they had a legitimate claim as potential heirs and successors.

As suggested in the discussion of type-two *bamli,* the designation of any heir and successor to an *alab* was made even more difficult because, with the one noted exception, the units included
the headmen's sons, maternal nephews, and in two cases, younger
brothers.

By 1964, ten years after the land division, three groups were
forced to make decisions because of the deaths of their *alab*. The
process was difficult, however, and disputes emerged over *alab*
rights and land.

Two of the deceased *alab* were heads of type-one *bamli*. One
was *alab* N, the head of *bamli* 3. As he was the last member of
his lineage (Makaoliej M 2), and the only adult males in his *bamli*
were his sons, there was never any doubt that his eldest son would
succeed him.

The death of the second *alab* of a type-one *bamli* resulted in
a dispute. The deceased was *alab* A of *bamli* 17. A was the head
of the junior Ijjirik lineage (I 3) who had challenged Juda's succession to the chieftainship with the vigorous support of his younger
brother. As described in Chapter Five, the families of both A and

his brother were originally allocated land together as *bamli* 7. Afterwards, the unity which the brothers had displayed earlier was dissolved when the younger brother forced *A* to withdraw from *bamli* 7. As a result, *A*, his wife, and adopted son became *bamli* 17, while the younger brother became one of the Kili headmen, *alab a.*

Prior to his death, *alab A* and his wife had adopted a second son and made him a member of their small *bamli*. *Alab A* stipulated that his land was to be divided between his two adopted sons, and each was to become *alab* on his own half of the estate. Upon *A*'s death, however, his brother claimed that he was *A*'s legitimate heir and successor on *bamli* 17's land because younger brothers had always succeeded elder ones.

A's widow asked that the dispute be mediated by chief Juda and the council who ruled that *A*'s adopted sons were his rightful successors. The issue was not resolved, however, since both claimants actually exploited the land. As *A*'s adopted sons were too young to defend their own interests, his widow enlisted her brothers to aid her in the collection of coconuts. Members of *alab a*'s *bamli* 7 also collected nuts from the land, but in view of adverse public opinion and admonitions from the council, they attempted to conceal their activity.

Alab a advanced other claims which were based on the former system of land rights with the same aggressiveness that he had exhibited earlier in support of his brother's claim to the chieftainship. With the death of his brother, he had become the head of the large junior Ijjirik lineage. As lineage head, he asserted that he was the rightful *alab* with authority over the land that had been allotted to the two *bamli,* numbers 8 and 19, headed by his maternal nephews. The latter defended their status as *alab* by embracing the new scheme of landholding and arguing that the former system pertained only to Bikini and the past. The council supported the nephews and again rebuffed *a*'s claims to authority over the land of other *bamli.*[2]

---

[2] One of *alab a*'s sister's sons was Bikini *alab C*, the recipient of the only parcel of gift land at Bikini in 1946. *C* could have also argued that he was a headman in his own right within the framework of the former system long before *a* became a headman on Kili.

Alab L, the head of the Makaoliej sub-clan and *bamli* 11, was the third *alab* who died by 1964. *Bamli* 11 was a type-two *bamli,* and as Table 7.2 reflects, it was originally composed of L's own children on Kili and his sister's children who were among the group of expatriates on Ailinglablab. Upon L's death, his next eldest brother, *alab o* of *bamli* 1, was recognized as L's successor as head of Makaoliej. He also laid claim to the *alab* rights of L's *bamli* land. Like *alab a,* he contended that younger brothers always succeeded elder ones as *alab* with authority over land. In contrast to the dispute over *A*'s land, however, L's sons were mature adults and were quite capable of defending their own interests. They flatly rejected *o*'s claim, and the latter did not pursue the issue. L's eldest son was recognized as his father's heir and successor. L's sister's sons were never present to contest the matter, and L's eldest son ceased to list them as *bamli* members.

The deaths of the three *alab* and their sons' succession to the status of *alab* at the head of their *bamli* units apparently influenced others to make decisions of their own. By 1964 the members of the thirteen type-one *bamli* and the type-two *bamli* 11 headed by L's son had concluded: " . . . sons will follow their fathers on Kili." In other words, they had adopted a patrilineal rule for the inheritance of *alab* rights and succession to the headship of the new landholding groups.

With the exception of *bamli* 11, no decisions regarding the future disposition of *alab* rights had been made by type-two *bamli.* The designation of any heir and successor to the headmen would only have created dissension within the groups. For the time being indecision was the easiest course of action.

Other Disputes. Disputes over *alab* rights other than those precipitated by death had also emerged by 1964. Two claims to the *alab* rights of *bamli* 12's land had been made. Originally, there were only four members in *bamli* 12: Kili *alab q,* the other two surviving members of the Makaoliej lineage segment M 3/3, and *q*'s son. Earlier, *q*'s ambition to become an *alab* on Kili had been supported by *alab c* of *bamli* 13 because of long standing relations between members of those two groups: (1) *q* and *c*'s wife were classificatory siblings and the latter had been adopted by the for-

mer's mother; (2) during the absence of the members of Makaoliej
M 3/3 from Bikini they had made *c* and his wife custodians on
their land.

Not long after the land division and as *alab c* had perhaps
anticipated *alab q* had once again left the community to return
to his former occupation as a wage earner on Kwajalein. Afterwards, *c* claimed that *bamli* 12's land fell under his authority.
To justify the claim, *c* had redefined the memberships of both
bamli. He no longer counted his wife as a member of his *bamli*
13 but contended that she belonged to *bamli* 12, and that he was
alab over the land to which his wife had rights.

Bikini *alab M*, head of Makaoliej lineage M 3/2–3/3 advanced
the second claim to *bamli* 12's land. The land to which the members of the lineage segment M 3/3 had rights at Bikini had been
under *M*'s authority (see discussion of Makaoliej sub-clan, Chapter
Three), and he argued that the former arrangement should be perpetuated on Kili. *M*, however, did not push his claim with any
resolve; *c* had the advantage in that his and *bamli* 12's allotments
were adjacent, and he actually used the land with his wife.

Other disputes over land resolved around boundary lines. In
two instances, members of one *bamli* charged that those of the
bamli holding land adjacent to theirs had made inroads into their
property by altering boundary markers cut into trees. A more
serious dispute erupted when one of the *alab* with land adjacent
to the abandoned taro swamp attempted to extend his allotment
by planting coconut trees on land in the swamp that had been
allocated to other *bamli* units in 1955.

Defining Bamli. While the majority of *bamli* groups had
made decisions about the inheritance of *alab* rights by 1964, the
Bikinians had not agreed upon a set of criteria for defining *bamli*
memberships after the groups were delineated for the land division.
Most Bikinians clung to notions derived from the former system
of land rights and believed that spouses should have access to one
another's land and that children should have some rights to the
land of both of their parents. No general agreement, however,
had been reached as to how recent marriages and births would
affect *bamli* membership.

In this unstructured situation, each *alab* had assumed the

prerogative of determining those he included as members of his *bamli*. As implied in the foregoing discussion of *alab* rights, this new prerogative provided the headmen with a new source of power, and some were employing it to extend their spheres of authority. In addition to those headmen who had altered *bamli* memberships in maneuvers pertaining to *alab* rights, their ability to offer *bamli* memberships was proving to be an effective means of manipulating the behavior of others. For example, one *alab* extended membership in his *bamli* to his daughter's estranged husband on the condition that he return to his wife and contribute to the *bamli*'s labor force. In some instances, the same enticement was offered to recently acquired spouses of the members of some *bamli* groups as the *alab* attempted to bring new affines within their spheres of authority.

The *alab* differed, however, in their decisions about extending membership in their respective units. In the case of all marriages which had occurred since the land division, the husbands and wives had retained membership in their original units. Some of the recently married couples and their children were counted in the membership of both the husbands' and wives' units. Others married since the division were not considered members of each other's *bamli*, but in some cases, their children were included as members of both parental units. By 1964 the husbands and wives who were married at the time of the division, but who were counted as members of different *bamli*, had been granted membership in their spouses' *bamli*. In some instances, their children held membership in both units, and in other cases they did not.

Thus, the *bamli* units were increasing in size, and their memberships had begun to overlap. One other factor also contributed to the increase in size of the units and, to a very small extent, to the overlapping of memberships. As noted, most islanders who had long been absent from the community were not included in the *bamli* units for the purpose of the land division. Afterwards, however, headmen began to list their expatriate kinsmen and the latter's relatives on other atolls as *bamli* members. While this had little immediate practical consequence, it had the effect of expanding the number of individuals over whom the *alab* claimed to have some authority.

As of 1964, 482 islanders were counted as members of the

nineteen *bamli*. Twenty-three married adults held membership in
two units, and twenty-nine children were included in the original
bamli of both their father and mother. Fifteen adopted children
held membership in the units of both their biological and adoptive parents. This represented a total of sixty-seven individuals
who were included in two *bamli*. Two of the children, however,
were counted as members of three (the original units of both
their father and mother as well as the *bamli* of an adoptive par-
ent) which increased the total overlap in the membership of the
bamli units to sixty-nine. Thus, 413 islanders comprised the nineteen *bamli*.

Bikini Alab and Kili Alab

The distinction between Bikini *alab* and Kili *alab* made at the
time of the land division was still clear in 1964. Six of the eleven
Bikini *alab* were still living. They and the men who were recognized as the legitimate heirs and successors to the five deceased
headmen were not reconciled to the redistribution of power and
influence that had occurred in the community and resented that
men of junior rank had gained authority over land and people on
Kili.

Tension between the two sets of headmen was evident in the
council. Three years after the land division, it was observed that
only Bikini *alab* or men recognized as their successors attended
meetings of the council (Mason 1958). They were attempting to
sustain the old authority structure, and they maintained that landholding on Kili did not warrant representation in the council.
They insisted that deceased Bikini *alab* were to be succeeded in
council by the men who would have inherited their land rights
and succeeded them as *alab* at Bikini. In spite of the resistance
of the Bikini headmen, the Kili *alab* gradually began to attend
the council sessions, and during the initial months of my own
fieldwork, all but one, and sometimes two, of the Kili *alab* actively participated in the council's deliberations.

My initial inquiries into the council organization rekindled
the antagonisms between the two sets of *alab*. The following
meeting of the council erupted in a stormy session in which the

Bikini *alab* demanded that the Kili *alab* leave. The latter defended their participation arguing that their status as *alab in brij* 'head of land' entitled them to seats in the council. I made no further inquiries about the council. Within two months, the Kili *alab* were once again attending council meetings, and with the exception of some grumbling, their presence went uncontested.

The disagreements over council membership were not unlike the disputes which had developed over the inheritance of *alab* rights on Kili. In the maneuvering for position, men chose between the former system of inheritance and succession and the new *bamli* system depending upon which provided a rationale for their respective ambitions. The Bikini *alab* clung to the old order; the Kili *alab* embraced the new.

In three cases where deceased Bikini *alab* were the last members of their respective lineages, there was, in fact, no conflict between the two systems. As previously discussed, two of the three Bikini *alab*, Lokwiar and *alab S,* had died before 1954, and their eldest sons were installed as councilmen prior to the land division. Since both sons also succeeded their fathers as household heads and were thus allotted Kili land, as *bamli* heads, they had become men with authority over land just as they would have at Bikini. Similarly, the death of Bikini *alab N* after the land division created no conflict regarding council membership. His eldest son not only inherited his father's rights as *alab,* but he also succeeded his father as a councilman as he would have at Bikini.

In the remaining two cases the old and new social orders were quite distinct. The younger brothers of the deceased *alab A* and *alab L* were recognized by the Bikini *alab* as their elder brothers' rightful successors in the council because at Bikini both would have inherited their brothers' *alab* rights and would have succeeded them as lineage heads. At the same time, the Bikini *alab* acknowledged that the adopted sons of *alab A* and the real sons of *alab L* were their fathers' legitimate heirs and successors on Kili.

The Bikinians' perception of the semi-annual interest payments from the trust fund functioned to reinforce the distinction between the Bikini *alab* and Kili *alab.* The islanders viewed the financial settlement as compensation for their loss of Bikini land.

Further, and with the probable urging of the Bikini *alab*, it was determined at the time of the first interest payment in 1957 that the Bikini *alab* were entitled to a larger share of the money than were the others because they always had a right to one-quarter of the copra receipts gained from the land. Accordingly, every Bikinian paid a small portion of his payment to the head of his lineage. Children born after relocation were considered members of their mother's corporate lineage just as they would have been at Bikini, and they also paid a portion of their share to its headman. In addition, siblings who had formed a patri-centered corporation with their father at Bikini paid him a portion of their share. In short, everyone paid a portion of the money received to the head(s) of the landholding group(s) to which he or she had belonged at Bikini. In the case of the Bikini *alab* who had died since relocation, the men who were recognized as their heirs and successors in the former system received the payments on Kili.[3]

Households and Landholding

By 1964 contrasts between Bikini and Kili landholding and settlement patterns as well as certain other events connected to the Bikinians' relocations had had notable effects upon patterns of residence and household formation. There was a total of twenty-one households. In contrast to Bikini where only one of eleven households had had less than eleven members, eleven of the twenty-one on Kili had ten or fewer residents. Eight other households numbered from thirteen to twenty-five people and were within the size range of most of those at Bikini in 1946. The remaining two groups were considerably larger than any of the past; one was Juda's which counted thirty-three individuals, and the other was the Jitoen headman's which had thirty-two.

Early in the Kili resettlement certain changes in the domestic groups had become apparent. Common interest to land at Bikini

---

[3] In 1963-64, each individual on the island received $13.00 from the interest payment (a decrease from the $16.75 received at the time of the first payment in July, 1957). From this amount, individual shares paid to the Bikini *alab* ranged from 50 cents to one dollar.

had functioned to hold kinsmen together in the households under the authority of the *alab*. With relocation, however, residential choices were no longer restrained by considerations of land or land rights, and several men other than the *alab* had established households of their own during the construction of the village on Kili (see Chapter Five). With the land division five years later, land rights again became a factor influencing choices of residence when the *alab* assumed the right of defining *bamli* membership and employed this new prerogative to influence the decisions of others.

It was quite evident, however, that rights to land were no longer so important for residence as they had been in former times. Three factors, of which only one was related directly to the changes in land rights and settlement pattern, accounted for the increase in the number of small domestic groups on Kili. First was that the compact village area was communal property— a crucial difference from the past. Members of relatively small family units within once larger extended and/or joint sibling households had the option of functioning as separate commensal units. This option had not been available when they were residing on land parcels under the authority of the *alab*. Some Bikinians were taking advantage of the new alternative; not all households were headed by an *alab,* and three were headed by males who had married into the community—a situation which could not have occurred in the past.

The second factor contributing to the increase in small households was the departure of some islanders to Kwajalein. Given the experience with outsiders and the improved image of themselves as well as a desire to find relief from Kili, residence at Kwajalein had become an alternative for some. Two males who had headed large households left Kili with the majority of their children and grandchildren, and only remnants of their former groups remained. Third, death had depleted other households, including those of two of the deceased Bikini *alab*.

The large size of the households of Juda and the Jitoen headman reflected the prominence both men had acquired since relocation. Most of their married children had elected to remain closely affiliated with the two centers of power and influence in the community, and they were members of their fathers' households. Together the two households formed a particularly influential entity in the community; their combined membership totalled sixty-five individuals, or twenty-three percent of the 282 islanders on Kili.[4]

Summary and Analysis

In the early 1960s the Bikinians were in the process of attempting to cope with problems inherent in the *bamli* landholding scheme they had implemented a decade earlier. The traditional matrilineal system of land rights and succession to the sta-

Plate 14. Chief Juda, 1963. *(Photo by Leonard Mason.)*

tus of *alab* was not congruent with the structure of the *bamli* corporations. As a result, the islanders had been forced to make decisions which were in the process of becoming new norms and procedures for defining how the rights of *alab* were to be inherited and how membership in the *bamli* units was to be determined.

The adoption of the patrilineal rule for the inheritance of *alab* rights by fourteen of the nineteen *bamli* represented the transfor-

---

[4] An extensive description of the households on Kili in 1964 is not required for the present study, but the data have appeared elsewhere (Kiste 1967; 1968).

mation into the prevailing norm of what had been formerly recognized as a common alternative to matriliny. This transformation may be accounted for by the interplay of new conditions, the traditional system and its alternatives, and the continuing motivation of self-interest. Thus, the Kili land division and *bamli* system created new opportunities to be exploited by those who gained thereby, while the shift to patrilineal succession could be rationalized in terms of the Bikini precedent of father-son succession and inheritance.

In retrospect, and given the structure of most of the *bamli* groups, it seems that only a brief time had to elapse after the Kili land division before sons were designated as their fathers' heirs and successors in the majority of the units. One of the *alab* succinctly summed up the situation: "Here on Kili, I provide for my own children because they are not with their mother's brother." The reluctance of the five groups which had yet made no decision regarding the future disposition of *alab* rights was understandable; given the structure of these groups, indecision avoided the dissension that would have been created within them by the designation of any heir and successor to the current *alab*.

Like the *bamli* scheme a decade earlier, the adoption of the patrilineal rule by the majority of *bamli* groups had consequences of which the Bikinians were not fully aware. The rule had, in effect, differentiated the rights of the children of the *alab* from those held by other *bamli* members. The children of the *alab*, particularly his sons, had become his designated successors whereas other *bamli* members were not potential *alab*.

After the 1963-64 research, I predicted that the patrilineal rule would influence the determination of *bamli* membership in the future. Assuming that males would be included as members of their fathers' groups as the latter's heirs and successors in the *bamli* which had adopted the patrilineal rule, males related by patrilineal descent would eventually comprise the core of each unit. It did not seem probable that a system of land tenure based on patrilineages would evolve for two reasons. First, the children of women who were married to males from other atolls would still have to be included in the *bamli* units. Secondly, if the Bikinians continued the trend of extending children's membership in both their mother's and father's *bamli,* the units might develop into some variety of non-unilineal descent groups with

alab rights being inherited patrilineally. Landholding groups of
a somewhat similar nature are found in the Gilbert Islands south
of the Marshalls and other societies in Oceania (cf. Goodenough
1955; Lundsgaarde and Silverman 1972).

The disputes over land, land rights, and statuses of authority
(including both disputes over succession to the status of *alab* and
the conflict over council membership) that had arisen on Kili represented a continuity with the past: the never ending competition
over these traditionally valued ends. Previously, alternatives within the traditional system of inheritance and succession had provided the primary basis for opposing claims as individuals and
groups maneuvered for advantage. On Kili, such maneuvers differed from the past only in that the islanders had two systems
available for manipulation. In disputes pertaining to the inheritance of *alab* rights, individuals chose between the old and new
systems depending upon which of the two offered the most advantage. Similarly, in matters pertaining to council membership,
the Bikini and Kili *alab* were clearly divided as the former attempted to perpetuate the system which had prevailed at Bikini
while the latter embraced the new order on Kili. All of the *alab*,
however, assumed the prerogative of defining the memberships of
their respective *bamli* groups; the newly acquired prerogative represented a further rejection of the former system, and some of
the *alab* were employing it quite obviously to increase their spheres
of influence.

Thus, the Bikinians had two models for the organization of
their community, and as they maneuvered for land and authority,
individuals and groups alternated between the two. The new order was manifest in the *bamli* corporations on Kili. The older order lived not only in memories of Bikini, but was given tangible
expression in the distribution of the semi-annual interest payments.

As further examination of details about the Kili *bamli* system
is not required for this study, it is appropriate here to comment
briefly upon findings derived from my 1969 research. Not enough
time had elapsed by 1969 to evaluate the accuracy of my earlier
predictions. The Bikinians had made no further progress in determining how *bamli* membership was to be defined, and with the
realization of their desire to have Bikini returned to them was the
possibility that problems pertaining to land on Kili would never
be resolved.

CHAPTER EIGHT

Return to Bikini

Responding to the Bikinians' failure to adjust to Kili and their pleas to be returned to their homeland, in the late 1960s the High Commissioner persuaded officials in Washington, D.C. to determine the condition of Bikini. The atoll on which no nuclear tests had been conducted since 1957 was examined by Atomic Energy Commission (AEC) scientists. In August, 1968 the President of the United States announced that with the exception of a few small islands, radiation levels were low enough that most of the atoll was safe for human habitation (U.S. Department of State 1968:304). The Bikinians were elated with the news, and shortly thereafter, several of them accompanied the High Commissioner, other officials, and a corps of newsmen on a reconnaissance of Bikini. The event was given wide coverage by the news media, and the Bikinians once again appeared in the pages of newspapers and magazines throughout the world.

The Bikinians' elation was dampened by what they saw. Bikini was not the idyllic homeland of their memories. A massive amount of debris and equipment left from the tests cluttered the islands and beaches. As a result of the nuclear experiments, two or three small islands and portions of others had disappeared. Most coconut palms and other plants of economic value had been removed or destroyed, and the atoll was engulfed by a dense layer of scrub vegetation.

Unfortunately, chief Juda who had led the community through the troubled years since relocation did not survive to learn that Bikini would be returned to his people; he died a few

Plate 15. Aerial view of Bikini Island, Bikini Atoll from the west, 1964. The lagoon is to right, and the ocean is in the foreground and horizon. All palm trees are gone; only scrub vegetation remains. *(Photo by Leonard Mason.)*

months before the Presidential announcement. Juda's son succeeded as head of his *bamli,* but the chief's death opened another chapter in the competition for power and influence in the community. The head of the junior Ijjirik lineage renewed his claim that Juda had never been the legitimate chief. From his point of view, the time had come for the rectification of past injustices, and because he was of superior generational standing within the structure of the Ijjirik sub-clan, he claimed the right to succeed to the chieftainship. Predictably, and as Juda and Lokwiar had done in earlier years, the Jitoen headman also claimed the chieftainship because he was a member of the senior ranking Ijjirik lineage.[1]

By 1968 both aspirants to the chieftainship were quite old. Because of their age and past self-assertiveness, neither had the confidence of their fellow islanders. The office of magistrate provided an alternative that had not been available in the past. The

---

[1] Like Juda, two more of the *alab* did not survive to learn of their impending return home. One was Kili *alab d,* the head of a type-one *bamli* who was succeeded by his son. The second, *alab C,* was one of the old Bikini *alab* who headed a type-two *bamli.* More than a year after his death, its members had yet to select a successor. With the deaths of Juda and *alab C,* only four of the eleven Bikini *alab* remained.

Bikinians thus elected Lokwiar's son to succeed Juda as magistrate and left the dispute over the chieftainship unresolved.

Rehabilitating Bikini

Officials of the Trust Territory, AEC, and agencies of the Department of Defense (DOD) planned the rehabilitation of Bikini in a two-phase program. First, the AEC and DOD had the relatively short-term but huge task of removing radioactive materials, other debris, and scrub vegetation, and in so far as possible, restoring the natural topography of islands. The Trust Territory assumed the responsibility for the second phase of the program involving the longer range tasks of replanting the atoll, constructing housing, and relocating the community. The two phases were to overlap since replanting was to commence with the removal of scrub vegetation.

Eniu, the second largest island in the atoll located south of the main island on the reef's eastern rim (see Map 3, page 17), was selected as the base of initial operations because it had an airstrip constructed during the test period. By early 1969 a tent village with an electrical power plant, a water distillation system, and a number of other modern conveniences were established on the island and weekly air service to Kwajalein was initiated. A task force of men outfitted with heavy equipment, a variety of vehicles, and LST's of World War II vintage began the cleanup operation. In June eight Bikini men were flown to the atoll to aid with the work.

It was projected that the actual resettlement would be accomplished over a period of eight or more years to allow for the maturation of newly planted palms and other subsistence crops. According to the administration's plan, work crews of men from Kili were to begin the planting under the direction of the Marshall Islands District Agricultural Department. The crews were to be employed by the administration and rotated every three months between Bikini and Kili so that men would not be separated from their families for extended periods of time. At an unspecified date, family units would gradually be relocated until the entire community was returned. Buildings were to be constructed of concrete block and aluminum roofing to avoid the same deterioration that had occurred on Kili. As an interim measure, $95,000 was budgeted to purchase materials for the renovation of the Kili village. The cost of the overall project was estimated at a sum far in excess of three million dollars.

By the time of my research in the summer months of 1969, much of the enthusiasm that had been generated by their project- ed return home had been dissipated, community morale was low, and the Bikinians were displeased with the rehabilitation program. The number of islanders on Kili had increased to 344; the birth rate remained unchecked, and relatives who had long been absent were returning. The increased population was more than the is- land could support, and the winter months of 1968-69 had been one of the worst the people had experienced. As in the past, on more than one occasion rough seas had prevented the landing of cargo. The USDA surplus foods had not been sufficient to tide the community over, the Cooperative's resources had been ex- hausted and it was bankrupt. Once again, before relief provisions were landed in the spring, the people had been reduced to a diet of immature coconuts.

As in earlier years, the Bikinians evoked the "milk and honey" image of Bikini and reiterated the hardships they had endured on Kili. After the much publicized announcement of their return home, they were dismayed that they had to remain on Kili for a few years to come. Many wanted to return to Bikini immediately and have the administration subsist them until newly planted trees matured. Those men who were and would be employed in the replanting program were demanding wages higher than those nor- mally paid to agricultural laborers. The people were also not sat- isfied with the plans for renovating the Kili village. Consistent with the stance they had taken in the past, they rejected the ad- ministration's assumption that they would provide the labor to rebuild their houses and insisted upon payment for their efforts.

The Bikinians, however, were hampered in their efforts to deal with the administration, because of the lack of strong leader- ship that Juda had provided, and because of the internal struggles for power which had divided the community into opposing fac- tions. Each of the aspirants to the chieftainship had his own co- terie of followers. Neither was supporting the new magistrate, and there was some indication that one of them was actively at- tempting to undermine the magistrate's authority as the head of

the community. The administration was either unaware or uncon-
cerned about the dispute over the chieftainship and officials were
dealing with the community through the new magistrate just as
they had formerly done with Juda. The magistrate was attempting to develop his own base of power and authority through his
status as a Bikini *alab,* his prestige as Lokwiar's son, the prominence gained by his role in the community's relocations, and the
support he was now receiving from officials as magistrate.

In August, 1969 the first shipment of seed nuts was taken
to Bikini and the Bikinians there began the planting program under the supervision of the Marshalls' district agriculturalist. The
cleanup phase of the program was completed in October. AEC,
military personnel, and much of their equipment were withdrawn
from the operation, the weekly air service to Kwajalein was terminated, and the program was turned over to the Trust Territory.
A special representative of the district administrator with experience in tropical agriculture was appointed to supervise the work
at Bikini. A crew of twenty-three workers from Kili and a second
load of seed nuts arrived at the atoll in December.

Phase two of the rehabilitation has been marked by serious
logistical problems which have impeded the program, and by the
Bikinians' attempts to gain further financial compensation and
other concessions from the Americans. The Bikinians' long standing concern over the amount of their interest payments was exacerbated when they learned that the displaced Enewetok people
were to receive a substantial financial award. The Enewetok people had remained on Ujelang since their resettlement there in 1947
(see Chapter Four). Like the Bikinians, they have always sustained the hope of returning to their homeland, and they too had received a trust fund as financial compensation. The impending return of the Bikinians to their homeland caused great unrest among
the Enewetok people, and they protested their continued alienation from Enewetok. In an effort to pacify them, "undisclosed
agencies" of the United States government provided them with
an *ex gratia* payment of $1,020,000 in 1969, and the funds were
invested for the community.[2] This action further convinced the

---

[2] In April, 1972 officials in Washington, D.C. announced that Enewetok Atoll would be returned to its people no later than the end of 1973. Recent
events indicate, however, that the actual date will be much later.

Bikinians that their settlement with the United States was inadequate. They renewed their appeals for an increase in their trust fund, and some suggested that they should demand restitution for Bikini land which had been damaged or destroyed.

Action soon followed, and during the winter of 1969-70 the Bikinians petitioned the High Commissioner for an immediate return to Bikini and further compensation in the amount of $100,000,000 for damages done to the atoll and the discomforts they had endured as a consequence of their relocation (Letter to High Commissioner from Kili Magistrate, December 14, 1969). In April, 1970 administration officials travelled to Kili to explain why the resettlement could not take place for a number of years. As an interim measure, the people were assured that every effort will be made " . . . to make living conditions on Kili more pleasant until Bikini is fit for habitation" (*Micronitor,* Vol. 1, No. 25, 1970). The sum of $10,000 was provided to reestablish the Cooperative, and Bikini men were employed by the administration to renovate the Kili village.

Not satisfied with the administration's responses to their requests, the Bikinians contacted the offices of a law firm on Guam in the summer of 1970 to explore the advantages of obtaining legal counsel. During the same period the workers at Bikini went on strike because they were dissatisfied with working conditions and believed that the task of clearing the atoll from debris was inadequately done. The strike was settled, but details are not available (*Micronitor* Vol. 1, Nos. 16 and 24, 1970).[3] In the fall of 1970 it was reported that almost every able-bodied adult male was employed by the administration to further the rehabilitation efforts at both Kili and Bikini. Shortly thereafter, the entire community was placed on a long-term relief food program.

Concern and disappointment over progress at Bikini, however, offset the satisfactions gained from these welfare efforts. While certain members of the Marshalls district administration, particularly those of the Agriculture Department, worked diligently in

---

[3] On more than one occasion, Marshallese stevedores have gone on strike at Majuro, and they may have served as an example which inspired the Bikinians to employ this tactic. I have no concrete data pertaining to the Bikinians' decision to seek legal counsel.

the effort to make the atoll habitable, it was obvious that phase
two of the project was neither progressing well nor receiving the
full support of the higher levels of the Territory administration.
For several months in 1970 and 1971, the only available vessel
for transportation between the base camp at Eniu and Bikini Island and pickup trucks for moving men, equipment, and seed nuts
were frequently out of repair. Because of erratic shipping and the
termination of the air service with Kwajalein, supplies and wages
for the workers arrived behind schedule. Several appeals to the
Office of the High Commissioner for logistic support and for the
services of a mechanic went unheeded. The program proceeded
at a snail's pace, but the replanting of Bikini and Eniu islands was
eventually completed. Plans for replanting other islands in the
atoll are vague or nonexistent.

 The Bikinians' first attempt to obtain legal counsel was unsuccessful. To press their claims for additional compensation and
to expedite the project at Bikini, they began to explore the possibility of obtaining assistance from the Micronesian Legal Services
Corporation (MLSC), an action-oriented agency established in the
Territory in 1971 and funded by the Office of Economic Opportunity. In May, 1973 the Directing Attorney for the MLSC in
the Marshalls petitioned the President of the United States to review the history and current status of the Bikinians.[4]

 In the fall of 1973 the administration announced that housing on Bikini was nearly completed, and, "If all is acceptable to
the people, the Trust Territory government is prepared to allow
them to return to Bikini Atoll permanently by Christmas this
year" (*Highlights* October 15, 1973). Thus, it appears that the
original plan for phase two of the rehabilitation project has been
significantly altered, and that the administration intends to return
the people to Bikini long before coconuts or other crops have
matured. Such a course of action will inevitably require that the
community continue to be subsidized for years to come.[5]

---

[4] The Directing Attorney received no response from officials in Washington,
D.C.

[5] In spite of the Trust Territory's optimistic announcement, the Bikinians
were not returned to their homeland in late 1973. The construction of hous-

Reevaluating Kili

The islanders' impending return to Bikini has caused some to reappraise Kili and the Jaluit lands. They are uncertain that they want to return to the remote atoll and indicate that they may prefer to remain on Kili. The latter alternative would be particularly attractive if the majority of people return to Bikini and leave Kili's copra resources for a relatively few. Younger islanders who have been born and raised on Kili are not familiar with lagoon fishing, sailing, or life on an atoll and some express reservations about abandoning the only home they have ever known.

Regardless of the ambivalence of some, all of the islanders want to maintain possession of Kili and the Jaluit lands. With regard to the former, they strongly believe that they have made too great an investment in the island to consider relinquishing it, and for all of its disadvantages, its coconut groves are admittedly of great value. While no actual use is being made of the Jaluit lands, the people's desire to keep them is just another reflection of their generalized concern over land.

Whether or not the Bikinians will retain Kili and the Jaluit lands is uncertain. The 1956 agreement with the United States provided the islanders with only full-use rights to the land until they are returned to Bikini (see Appendix). The administration has remained silent on the issue, and it appears that the future disposition of Kili and the Jaluit lands will be determined through negotiation.[6]

The return of Bikini to the people, the possibility of keeping Kili and the Jaluit lands, and the hope that further financial compensation may be forthcoming has roused the interests of those islanders who have long been absent from the community.

---

ing was not completed in time. Other factors contributing to the delay are unknown, and as this study goes to press no firm date for the Bikinians' return to their atoll has been set.

[6] As in earlier years, negotiations with Americans are conducted through interpreters, a procedure with great potential for misunderstanding. A few younger Bikinians have acquired a fair command of English through the school system, but very few individuals over thirty years of age are fluent in the foreign language.

Shortly after the 1968 Presidential announcement, some of the expatriates began to reestablish their ties by returning to their relatives on Kili, and thus helped increase the number of islanders on Kili to 344. Despite the return of some, the number of relatives on other atolls had continued to increase to a total of 196 by new births and additional marriages to other islanders. Thus, by 1969 the total number of individuals who could claim some right to Bikini had risen to 540, more than twice the number in 1946 (see Tables 3.1 to 3.4, pages 39-42).

The trend has continued; more expatriates, their descendants, and their relatives have joined the community on Kili, and in 1973, the island's population numbered over 400.

The Paramount Chief

Predictably, the return of Bikini has rekindled the paramount chief's interest in the atoll. He never accepted the Americans' offer of financial compensation for his loss of Bikini, and in terms of Marshallese tradition and the policies of the successive colonial governments in the islands, he can claim that the atoll is a legitimate part of his domain. To date, the chief has remained in the background and has made no demands for restoration of his former rights. He is, however, attempting to gather support from among the expatriates, particularly those who settled on Ailinglablab Atoll. While the extent of his success is uncertain, it is known that some of the expatriates who have joined the community on Kili include members of the Ailinglablab group. They are currently attempting to persuade others to accept once again the paramount chief's hegemony over them.

Having ended their subordinate status to the chief, it is certain that the majority of Bikinians will reject his efforts to regain his former position. The chief has little to offer them, and the people view him as a potential drain on their resources. They have cast their lot with the United States.

Recent political developments, however, may threaten Bikinians' dependence upon the United States. In response to pressures from the United Nations and growing Micronesian criticisms of the American administration of the Trust Territory, in 1969 the United States began negotiations with Micronesians to determine the future political status of the islands. It appears that Micronesia will eventually choose between two alternatives: a Micronesian nation joined in free association with the United States or independence. Although no final agreements have been reached, it appears that under the first alternative, Micronesia would be self-governing in internal affairs. The United States would provide financial support and manage international affairs. In return, Micronesian lands would be available to the United States for the development of military bases and strategic facilities (Wenkam and Baker 1970:168). An independent state, however, would have no guarantees of economic assistance.

While the future political status of the Trust Territory is uncertain, there is little doubt that in the not too distant future Micronesians will assume the responsibility of managing at least their own domestic affairs. When this occurs, the American agencies upon which the Bikinians have become so dependent will be withdrawn from the islands. There is no reason to assume that a newly formed Micronesian government will feel obliged to take on responsibility for the Bikinians' welfare and continued rehabilitation of Bikini Atoll. The Bikini situation is viewed as a problem that Americans have created and for which Americans are entirely responsible. At the same time, the Bikinians have no long-term commitment from the United States, and they may be forced to fall back upon themselves.

CHAPTER NINE

Summary
and Conclusions

On Bikinians

The preceding eight chapters have focused largely upon the
Bikinians. The islanders' relocations have been described, and the
modifications that have occurred in the organization of their community and its relations with outsiders have been examined. Analyses of events have been provided throughout the study and
need not be repeated here. This section is a summation of the
study's most salient aspects. The closing section concerns other
issues pertaining to the United States administration of the Trust
Territory over the past quarter century.

The modifications of the Bikini community's internal organization and its altered relations with Americans and the paramount
chief may be largely attributed to competition over the distribution of power, influence, privilege, and control of valued resources.
The pre-European history of both the community and the Marshall Islands as a whole reveals that motivations to gain advantage
in the pursuit of these related interests were not recent or were
they introduced with relocation. Rather, these motivations are
an integral and enduring facet of Marshallese culture and society.
Traditionally, competition was focused on land and those social
statuses which entailed authority over land. This authority provided some with power and influence as well as special privileges.
Before armed conflict was terminated by the German colonial
government and the mission effort, the pursuit of advantage was

manifest in and accounted for the intra-community hostilities at Bikini and inter-atoll warfare waged elsewhere in the islands by competing paramount chiefs. With the introduction and spread of the copra trade, land became more valuable, and chiefs and heads of landholding corporations gained further power and privilege when they became entitled to larger shares of the cash receipts. Competition over rights to land continued after warfare had ended in less overt forms of maneuvering within the framework of alternative principles of succession and inheritance available in the traditional culture.

In one sense, the Bikinians' relocations have just been another set of circumstances, albeit a unique and extraordinary one, that could be employed in the pursuit of traditional ends. While contact with Americans and more acculturated Marshallese stimulated the Bikinians to question the traditional social order, other factors have been of much greater importance in determining their responses to their relocations. The necessity of reestablishing residences and allocating land on another island provided the opportunity to challenge the old order for men who occupied positions of advantage within the traditional social structure or who had other means of advancing their ambitions. Some men were clearly more aggressive than others in furthering their own interests because of their temperament and personality. The competition over land on Kili resulted in a land division which brought about a redistribution of power, influence, and privilege and a concomitant reorganization of the entire community.

The landholding corporations created by the division of Kili are qualitatively different from the matrilineal and patri-centered ones of the past. The majority of the new corporations are cognatic structures and, therefore, are not congruent with traditional matrilineal rules for determining succession and inheritance. The adoption of a patrilineal rule of succession and inheritance of headmen's rights on Kili is workable given the structure of the groups and represents a transformation of what had been a common alternative to matriliny into the prevailing norm for the majority of the corporations. Both the patrilineal rule and the headmen's recently assumed prerogative of defining the membership of their respective groups, represent a conscious rejection of the old order.

In addition to the perquisites traditionally associated with authority over land, the introduction of the council form of government; the support and recognition that Americans have given those who have occupied council offices; and the roles played by four men during the relocations have added new elements which are and have been employed in the competition for familiar ends. The council provided the traditional leaders of the community with official status in the American administrative apparatus. The right to be represented in the council has been a source of contention between the Bikini and Kili headmen, and the office of magistrate has become firmly established as a political prize. The late chief Juda utilized the advantages associated with this office as well as the prominence he gained from the events of relocation to enhance his position in the community when his legitimacy as chief was challenged and the traditional basis for chiefly power and influence had been largely eroded. More recently, Lokwiar's son began drawing upon the advantages of his incumbency as magistrate and the prominence he gained as council scribe along with the support he can garner from his status in the traditional social order. As recent events suggest, the offices of magistrate and hereditary chief have become separated. It seems clear that the office of magistrate will emerge as the more powerful and thus more sought after position, and if a successor to Juda is not named, it is possible that the chieftainship may cease to exist.

The importance of the head *(alab M)* of the large junior Makaoliej lineage has not increased as much as that of Juda or Lokwiar's son, but *alab M*'s ascendency in community affairs and his selection as scribe reflect the influence and prominence he gained because of his role in the relocations and status in the traditional system.

In contrast to the above three men, the Jitoen headman's enlarged sphere of authority on Kili is derived more from other factors than his position as one of the council's officers (policeman). On the strength of his own forceful personality and his status as Juda's second in command within the traditional order, he had begun to emerge as a more influential figure at Rongerik. The realignment of the spatial relationships of households on Kili provided him with the opportunity to establish himself as the head of one of the two village districts.

Regarding the Bikinians' relations with figures external to their community, issues pertaining to the paramount chief have revolved largely around traditional affairs. The chief did not possess resources sufficient to fulfill his obligation to appreciably assist the Bikinians in times of need, and moreover, there is no evidence that he made any significant effort to do so. On the contrary, his initial desire to have the Bikinians resettled within his domain, his later attempt to acquire title to Kili, and his recent use of expatriates to influence islanders on Kili reveal that his primary and consistent objective has been the preservation of his own authority over the people and a right to a portion of their resources.

For the Bikinians, a once isolated people, the initial contact with Americans after World War II and the events of their relocations have represented dramatic manifestations of the wealth in material resources and technological prowess of the United States. The islanders' experiences created wants for material goods which could not be satisfied by traditional means. As early as the Rongerik relocation, some Bikinians recognized that their only hope of returning to Bikini and perhaps gratifying these new found wants depended upon ending their relationship to the chief and establishing a dependent stance upon and acquiring some influence over the United States. Accordingly, and since the early days of their initial relocation, the Bikinians' management of their relations with the paramount chief and Americans has been designed to achieve these ends.

The Bikinians have employed a range of tactics in the pursuit of their objectives over the years. Initially, they were uncertain as to how to deal with the Americans and the paramount chief, and they had little leverage which could be brought to bear upon them. In their early attempts to rid themselves of the chief and attach themselves to the United States, they turned to their own history to reinterpret and give new emphases to certain past events. They denied that the chief had ever established his authority over Bikini, and recalled and elaborated upon his alleged failures to fulfill his obligations in the past. Early events of their relocations were employed to advance their arguments, and the claim that the navy promised to care for them indefinitely appears to have been at least some distortion of whatever commitments were made in 1946.

Many of the welfare measures implemented on behalf of the people at Rongerik, Kwajalein, and in the later years on Kili have represented tacit admission that because of their relocations by the Americans they have indeed been made to suffer discomfort and deprivation. The administration's periodic concern over their plight has served to reaffirm the Bikinians' conviction that they have been the victims of a great injustice, and they have made the most of the issue in their constant flow of petitions and pleas for aid and relief on Kili and a return to Bikini. Even though the islanders' frequent appearances at the offices of the district administration came to be disparagingly labelled as "the usual Kili recreation," the Bikinians' tenacity and persistence have served to make the "Bikini problem" a perpetual thorn in the administration's side and have been an important facet of their effort to achieve their objectives. Ironically, each welfare measure provided by the Americans has only reaffirmed the Bikinians' belief that the United States possesses unbounded power and resources and thus sustained their efforts to acquire greater influence over American actions.

Recent events not only indicate that the Bikinians' strategies have produced some of their desired results, but they also reflect the experience and sophistication acquired in dealing with Americans and the degree to which the Bikinians have been able to influence administration policies. In fact, the use of the technique of the workers' strike at Bikini in 1970 and the islanders' recent exploration of the potential advantages in obtaining legal counsel indicate that they are discovering more direct and effective devices to gain influence and, in reference to particular goals, perhaps legal power over the administration. Given the uncompleted rehabilitation of Bikini Atoll and absence of any firm long-term commitment from the United States, these newly found techniques may well be required if the Bikinians are to realize a return to a Bikini capable of supporting their increased numbers. Recourse to legal action may be needed as they attempt to gain additional financial compensation, and, perhaps, maintain possession of Kili and the Jaluit lands.

During the islanders' years on Kili, Bikini and Kili have become important symbols with multiple and conflicting meanings in both the internal and external affairs of the community. The image of Bikini as a "land of milk and honey" and the representation of Kili as a "calaboose" have been employed to express the Bikinians' feelings and desires in their dealings with Americans. Bikini has clearly come to represent all that they have been deprived of whereas Kili represents all their felt grievances and injustices. Both images will undoubtedly continue to be evoked when advantageous in negotiations with Americans, but among themselves the impending return to Bikini has caused the islanders to reassess these symbols. In contrast to the image of a land of plenty, Bikini's remoteness and relatively poor agricultural potential are now being more critically evaluated. The positive attributes of Kili, its proximity to the district center at Majuro, and its coconut groves are being reconsidered. This reevaluation of the symbols which have played such an important part in the minds of Bikinians over the past twenty-five years is a reflection of the ambivalence that some now display about their return to Bikini.

Regarding internal affairs, Bikini and Kili also serve as symbols for the two models that the islanders now have for the organization of their community. For those who enjoyed positions of advantage within the framework of the traditional system, Bikini represents a condition of the past where political and economic relations were in their proper alignment, whereas Kili is a reminder of the present order where proper social relations have been corrupted and rightful power and influence have been diminished. In contrast, for those men who have achieved the perquisites associated with authority over land as a consequence of relocation, Bikini is a symbol of an age when only a few enjoyed the advantages of these valued ends, while Kili represents a more desirable social order which should be perpetuated.

As Bikini is returned to the people, and as they maneuver to maintain possession of Kili and the Jaluit lands and obtain more financial compensation, the competition among the islanders will inevitably enter a new phase. The models that the Bikinians now have for the organization of their community will exacerbate the existing division between those who have a vested interest in revitalizing the traditional system and those who have gained advantage by the new order on Kili. If events of the past permit conjecture about the future, it seems reasonable to predict that men other than the Bikini and Kili headmen will attempt to capitalize upon the resettlement of Bikini in order to advance their own interests just as the Kili headmen did in the past. Further, the expatriates who are joining the community after long years of absence are obviously concerned with representing their own interests and can be expected to enlarge the scope of the competition. As the reoccupation of Bikini becomes a reality and as the islanders pursue those ends which have always been manifest in their history and behavior, it may well be that neither the traditional system nor the new one on Kili will serve to order political and economic relations among them, and that another reorganization of the community will occur.

A Note on the Governing of Men

The Bikinians of today are a much more sophisticated and experienced people than those who left their homeland in 1946. They have learned to deal with Americans in increasingly effective ways, and they are no longer the shy and uncertain people of the past. The price the Bikinians have paid for their recently gained worldliness has been high, and it is not difficult to share their conviction that they have indeed suffered a great injustice and that the United States has an obligation to them. For the past quarter century, those islanders who knew Bikini Atoll well have experienced mental anguish and physical deprivation. Those who were young at the time of relocation or were born afterwards have paid the psychic cost of growing up in a community whose elder members were discontent and frustrated with their lot.

The future will also be difficult. The return to Bikini will require major adjustments for all. For older islanders, the Bikini of today is radically altered from the homeland they left. The younger people have much to learn about life on a remote atoll, and in a very real sense, they are the second generation of islanders to be relocated from an environment with which they are familiar.

The misfortune of the Bikinians would perhaps seem less tragic if it were an isolated case. At the time the United States gained control of the islands, twenty-five of the thirty-four atolls and single islands which comprise the Marshalls were inhabited.[1] Of the twenty-five, people of six have been adversely effected in very direct ways by American post-war military operations.

As noted, the people of Enewetok were relocated in 1947 because their atoll became the United States' second nuclear test site in the Pacific. Preliminary plans for returning the Enewetok people to their homeland are now being formulated but only after recent legal proceedings became embarrassing for the United States Air Force and caused it to end the testing of non-nuclear explosions on the atoll (*Pacific Islands Monthly* Vol. 44, No. 7, July, 1973). It is unlikely, however, that actual resettlement will occur in the near future.

Brief reference to the fate of the Rongelab people was made in Chapter Six. On March 1, 1954, unexpected winds carried radioactive particles from a nuclear test at Bikini eastward toward Rongelab and Uterik Atolls. Both populations were evacuated to Kwajalein. Uterik suffered far less fallout than did Rongelab, and its people were returned home after two months. The "snowlike" fallout which fell upon Rongelab made it unsafe for human occupancy, and its people were moved to Majuro. They resided there for over three years during which time they were provided with food, housing, medical attention, and monetary compensation for the copra they would have made at home.

The Rongelabese were returned home to a village newly constructed by the Americans in late June, 1957. The three-year period of enforced dependence deprived them of both opportunities and incentives to care for themselves, and they were not prepared to return to their former self-sufficiency. Food subsidies were continued for another two years, and by 1959, the Rongelabese " . . . were not ready, or did not know how, to take charge of their lives again" (Hines 1962:258). Like the Bikinians, the Rongelabese had been seduced into a state of dependence upon the United States, and the financial compensation of $900,000 provided a short time later further inclined them to become wards

---

[1] The uninhabited atolls were Taongi, Bikar, Taka, Erikub, Rongerik, Ailinginae, and Ujelang; the uninhabited islands were Jemo and Kili. With the exception of Ujelang, the uninhabited atolls were like Rongerik and did not have resources sufficient to support communities of any substantial size.

of the Americans. Other long-term consequences of the nuclear
tests upon the people are uncertain. They receive annual medical
examinations; a high frequency of thyroid disorders and one death
have apparently been linked to the people's exposure to excessive
radiation.

In the early 1960s the people of Lib Island a short distance
to the south of Kwajalein became endangered by debris falling
from intercepted missiles exploding in the area. They were resettled on Ebeye Island within Kwajalein Atoll and were given total
care similar to that provided for the Rongelabese during their Majuro sojourn. By the mid-1960s Lib no longer fell within the endangered area, a new village was constructed for the people, and
they were returned home. The former life style of the community
had been disrupted, however, and many islanders did not return
to Lib. Other consequences of their dislocation have not been
discerned.[2]

The lives of the people of Kwajalein were disrupted before
the arrival of the Americans when Japan fortified the atoll before
World War II. The United States military occupied the Japanese-
held land; the main island became the principal base of operations,
and several other islands were established as support facilities. As
the atoll was developed as a missile test site, those people who had
remained on their home islands within Kwajalein were, like the
Lib people, moved to Ebeye for their own safety. In contrast to
the opulent American community on the main island, Ebeye is an
overcrowded shanty town with an inadequate water supply and
poor sanitary and health conditions. The dislocated people are
paid for the copra that they cannot produce. Those who have
rights to the main island received financial compensation (see Chapter Six), but others who have been dispossessed have gained nothing from their lost land.

Elsewhere in the Trust Territory, the direct effects of American military interests have been most apparent in the Marianas. Islands of that district remained under the control of the navy from
World War II until the early 1960s. During that period, large sec-

---

[2] The available information on the relocation of the Lib people is meager,
and it appears that it was never revealed in the United States annual reports
to the United Nations.

tions of Saipan Island were closed off and used by the Central Intelligence Agency for the training of Nationalist Chinese troops.

Other Micronesians have also been effected, albeit less directly, by the defense interests of the United States. During the first eighteen years of the American administration, the United States took an ambivalent position toward the Territory. For strategic reasons, America maintained firm control over the islands, and private citizens were allowed to enter the area only with navy security clearance. At the same time, the United States had no commercial or other nonmilitary interest in the islands, and as long as American defense interests were served, the Territory administration was allowed to operate in a policy vacuum. No plans were developed for the future of the islands, and areas that were severely damaged by the war were not rehabilitated. The administration limped along on meager budgets since the United States Congress set an appropriations ceiling of $7.5 million a year for the entire Territory, and actual funds allotted never averaged even that amount throughout the first decade of American rule (Wenkam and Baker 1971:162).

As in the case of the Bikinians' ordeals at Rongerik and Kili, the United States did not respond to general conditions in the Territory until outside pressures were exerted. During the latter 1950s the United Nations became increasingly impatient with the few steps that had been taken to lead the islanders to self-government. In response, the United States began a program for strengthening district legislatures and committed itself to the development of a Territory legislature.

The year 1962 marked a turning point. An investigating committee commissioned by President Kennedy reported that conditions in the islands were deplorable. The Kennedy administration obtained the first raise in the ceiling on appropriations, and spending rose to $17.2 million by fiscal year 1964. A crash program was begun. Health facilities were upgraded, a large school construction effort was launched, and American teachers were recruited to staff the new classrooms. Annual budgets were expanded to over $50 million by the early 1970s. The funds increased the size of government agencies and created jobs for Micronesians, and a greater number of islanders began to enjoy a nontraditional life style which depended upon the consumption of imported goods and American financial support.

In 1966 President Johnson sent the Peace Corps to the Territory. Most of the volunteers have taught English as a secondary language in the schools, and consequently the number of islanders with a workable knowledge of the language has grown substantially. In the late 1960s military construction teams went to the Territory to augment the administration's hardpressed public works staff, to speed work on roads and other facilities, and to train some islanders in the operation of construction equipment (Ibid. 164-169).

In retrospect, it is apparent that the programs implemented in the 1960s were designed to both Americanize and make Micronesians dependent upon the United States so that the latter could maintain its hegemony over the area. As the day for determining their own future political status approaches, the islanders are in the position of having become accustomed to public services and to an economy that they cannot sustain with their own resources.

The Congress of Micronesia, the territory-wide legislature which was promised in the late 1950s and became a reality in 1965 (see Meller 1969), has appointed a commission to negotiate with representatives of the United States. By forming a united front and capitalizing upon American desires to maintain bases in the islands, Micronesians potentially had considerable bargaining power to bring to the conference table. However, Micronesian unity has always been fragile because of significant cultural differences among the islanders and because resources are not equally distributed among the islands. Further, the United States has encouraged separatism by opening yet other negotiations with the people of the Marianas where military interests are now focused. With the withdrawal of troops from Southeast Asia, the Marianas offer the United States a good defense perimeter in the Western Pacific; some of the people of the Marianas favor such a development, and their islands may become a permanent possession of the United States.[3] If this occurs, American military

---

[3] The people of the Marianas, known as Chamorros, are the most Westernized of all Micronesians. Contact occurred early, and the traditional culture

needs, with the possible exception of Kwajalein, will be satisfied; other Micronesians will be left with little to negotiate, and their fate may be largely determined by Americans.

The case of the Bikinians as well as those of the other populations discussed above have obvious parallels in the United States' relations with other societies, particularly those which were indigenous to North America. In the Pacific as well as North America, Americans have assumed a cultural and racial superiority which they believe justifies their disruption of the lives of dark-skinned peoples and the seizure of the latter's real estate for American ends. The manner in which restitution is sometimes attempted offers another similarity; after-the-fact provision of financial compensation and other poorly conceived welfare measures appear to ease the conscience of Americans and allow them to avoid examining the consequences of their acts. While Americans and Bikinians both act in terms of their own advantage, there is one very obvious and crucial difference between them; the former comprise a large and powerful society that has accepted the responsibility to protect the welfare of the other which is small and relatively powerless. With regard to that responsibility, the United States' record in Micronesia speaks for itself. The future of Micronesia does not appear very promising, and the American attitude toward the area and its people may well have been summed up by Presidential advisor (now Secretary of State) Henry Kissinger: "There are only 90,000 people out there. Who gives a damn?" (Hickel 1971: 191).[4]

---

was destroyed by the Spanish in the sixteenth and seventeenth centuries. For the Chamorros, the military establishment offers opportunities for employment and a general economic boom.

[4] Kissinger's remarks were made in 1969. By mid-1972, the Territory's population was about 115,000 (*Trust Territory of the Pacific Islands 25th Annual Report to the United Nations* 1972).

Appendix

TRUST TERRITORY OF THE PACIFIC ISLANDS
Majuro, Marshall Islands

November 22, 1956

AGREEMENT IN PRINCIPLE REGARDING
THE USE OF BIKINI ATOLL

WHEREAS, in order for the Trust Territory of the Pacific Islands to play its part in the maintenance of international peace and security it became necessary for the United States of America, the administering authority for the said Trust Territory, to occupy and use, with the consent of the inhabitants, all of the atoll of Bikini located in the Marshall Islands, between 11 degrees 29 minutes North latitude to 11 degrees 43 minutes North latitude, and 165 degrees 11 minutes East Longitude to 165 degrees 34 minutes East longitude, thus depriving the owners of the use of said atoll;

WHEREAS, an assembled meeting was held on Kili Island on November 9, 1956, with the majority of the people who possess rights in Bikini Atoll to discuss a settlement for the past and future use of Bikini Atoll, and

WHEREAS, agreement was reached at said meeting with no one present dissenting,

It is hereby agreed as follows:

1. The Government of the Trust Territory of the Pacific Islands will grant and convey to all of the people who possess land rights in Bikini Atoll, that is the commoners, according to the accepted Marshallese custom, full use rights in the following islands, islets and land parcels from the public domain of the said Trust Territory:

Kili, also known as Hunter's Island, located at 5 degrees
  38 minutes 45 seconds North latitude and 169 degrees
  7 minutes East longitude;
Jebet (Devet) located on the eastern side of the Jaluit

Atoll at 6 degrees 7 minutes 46 seconds North
latitude and 169 degrees 33 minutes 43 seconds
East longitude;
Jar (Djar) located on the eastern side of Jaluit Atoll at
6 degrees 7 minutes 36 seconds North latitude and
169 degrees 33 minutes 46 seconds East longitude;
Bokalablab located on the eastern side of Jaluit Atoll at
6 degrees 6 minutes 50 seconds North latitude and
169 degrees 35 minutes 10 seconds East Longitude;
and the land area on the southern end of Jabwor Island
located on the eastern side of Jaluit Atoll known as
Lojokar. All government lands south of Lojokar
wāto to the end of Lullol wāto.

All these lands may be divided among the former Bikini people as
they shall mutually agree, and the use rights to the land, lagoon, or
reefs of the above mentioned lands, together with all buildings and
trees thereon shall be held by them, and their heirs and assigns in
accordance with the accepted Marshallese customs.

2. The aforesaid use rights in the aforesaid government lands
shall continue until such time as it may be possible for the people
to return to Bikini, providing they wish to return to occupy said Atoll.

3. The Government of the Trust Territory of the Pacific Islands
and/or Government of the United States of America shall possess the
full use rights to Bikini Atoll until such time as it determines it will
no longer be necessary to occupy and use the said Atoll.

4. The sum of $325,000 shall be conveyed to those persons,
those commoners, who possess rights in Bikini Atoll. This money is
to be administered as follows: (1) $25,000, receipt of which is here-
by acknowledged, to be paid the aforesaid parties at the time of signing this agreement and may be divided among those who possess aforesaid rights in Bikini Atoll, or otherwise utilized as all parties concerned
agree; and (2) the remaining $300,000 to be placed in a trust fund to
be established and administered by the High Commissioner until such
time as said trust fund can be administered by a qualified institution.
The trust fund shall be invested only in United States Government se-
curities and interest accrued from said fund will be paid in such manner as may be further agreed upon by the *alabs* and people with vested
land rights in Bikini.

5. The people and *alabs* signing this Agreement in Principle represent that they have the full and complete right to represent the interests of any and all individuals who by reason of having lived on Bikini or Kili, may now or at any future date have a claim against the
United States or Trust Territory Governments by reason of their use
of Bikini Atoll.

Accordingly, the people and *alabs* signing this agreement agree that any future claims by Bikinians based on the use of Bikini by the Governments of the United States or the Trust Territory or on the moving of the Bikini people from Bikini Atoll to Kili Island shall be against them and not against the Government.

This Agreement was made voluntarily and without any compulsion or coercion whatsoever.

Bibliography

BOOKS AND ARTICLES

Alkire, William H.
    1972   *An Introduction to the Peoples and Cultures of Micronesia.*
               Reading, Mass.: Addison-Wesley.

Bryan, E.H. Jr.
    1972   *Life in the Marshall Islands.* Honolulu: Pacific Science Infor-
               mation Center, Bernice P. Bishop Museum.

Carroll, Vern
    1970   "Introduction: What Does 'Adoption' Mean?" In *Adoption
               in Eastern Oceania* (ed. Vern Carroll). Association for Social
               Anthropology in Oceania Monograph no. 1. Honolulu: Uni-
               versity of Hawaii Press.

Drucker, Philip
    1950   *The Ex-Bikini Occupants of Kili Island.* Pearl Harbor: Type-
               script.

Erdland, A.
    1914   *Die Marshall-Insulaner.* Anthropos: Internationale Sammlung
               Ethnologischer Monographien, vol. 2, no. 1. Munster.

Geertz, Clifford
    1957   "Ritual and Social Change: A Javanese Example." *American
               Anthropologist* 59:1.

Goodenough, Ward H.
    1955   "A Problem in Malayo-Polynesian Social Organization." *Amer-
               ican Anthropologist* 57:1.

Hickel, Walter J.
    1972   *Who Owns America?* New York: Coronet Communications,
               Paperback Library.

Highlights
    1973   A bi-monthly newsletter published by Public Information
            Office, U.S. Trust Territory of the Pacific Islands, October
            15, 1973.

Hines, Neal O.
    1962   *Proving Ground: An Account of the Radiobiological Studies
            in the Pacific, 1946-1961.* Seattle: University of Washington
            Press.

Honolulu Star-Bulletin
    1946   April 1.

Jeschke, C.
    1906   *Bericht uber die Marshall-Inseln.* Petermanns Mitteilungen
            52:272-73.

Kiste, Robert C.
    1967   *Changing Patterns of Land Tenure and Social Organization
            Among the Ex-Bikini Marshallese.* Ph.D. dissertation, Uni-
            versity of Oregon. (Available from University Microfilms, A
            Xerox Company, Ann Arbor, Michigan.)

    1968   *Kili Island: A Study of the Relocation of the Ex-Bikini Mar-
            shallese.* Eugene: Department of Anthropology, University
            of Oregon.

    1972   "Relocation and Technological Change in Micronesia." *Tech-
            nology and Social Change* (ed. H. Russell Bernard and Pertti
            Pelto). New York: Macmillan.

Kiste, Robert C. and Michael A. Rynkiewich
    forth- "Incest and Exogamy: A Comparative Study of Two Marshall
    coming Island Populations." In *Incest Prohibition in Polynesia and
            Micronesia* (ed. Vern Carroll). Association for Social Anthro-
            pology in Oceania Monograph. Honolulu: University of Ha-
            waii Press.

Leach, E.R.
    1954   *Political Systems of Highland Burma.* Boston: Beacon Press.

Leysne, Humphrey W.
    1952   "Food for Kili." *Micronesian Monthly* (forerunner of *High-
            lights*). U.S. Trust Territory of the Pacific Islands.

Life Magazine
    1946   "Atom Bomb Island: Navy Moves Natives from Bikini, Target
            of Operation Crossroads." *Life* 20 (March 25): 105-109.

Lundsgaarde, Henry P. and Martin G. Silverman
    1972   "Category and Group in Gilbertese Kinship: An Updating of Goodenough's Analysis." *Ethnology* XI: 2.

MacMillan, Howard G.
    1947   *Rehabilitation for the Marshallese Natives of Rongerik.* Kwajalein, Marshall Islands: Typescript.

Mair, Lucy
    1965   "How Small-scale Societies Change." *Penguin Survey of the Social Sciences 1965* (ed. Julius Gould). Baltimore: Penguin.

Markwith, Carl
    1946   "Farewell to Bikini." *National Geographic Magazine* 90 (July): 97-116.

Mason, Leonard
    1947   *Economic and Human Resources, Marshall Islands.* United States Commercial Co., Economic Survey of Micronesia, vol. 8. Typescript (Microfilm copy in the Library of Congress).

    1948   *Rongerik Report.* Honolulu: Typescript.

    1950   "The Bikinians: a transplanted population." *Human Organization* 9 (Spring): 5-15.

    1954   *Relocation of the Bikini Marshallese: A Study in Group Migration.* Ph.D. dissertation, Yale University.

    1958   "Kili Community in Transition." *South Pacific Commission Quarterly Bulletin* 18 (April): 32-35.

McKnight, Robert K.
    1960   *Competition in Palau.* Ph.D. dissertation, Ohio State University.

Meade, Lt. (J.G.) Herbert C., U.S.N.R.
    1946   *Operation Crossroads: Resettlement of Bikini Population.* Report on Administration of Military Government for the Month of March, by the Island Commander, Kwajalein, to Commander, Marianas. Mimeographed.

Meller, Norman
    1969   *The Congress of Micronesia.* Honolulu: University of Hawaii Press.

Micronitor
    1970   Weekly newspaper printed in the Marshall Islands, vol. 1, nos. 16, 24, and 25.

Milne, James
    1955   *Kili Project Report (Final).* Majuro, Marshall Islands: Type-
            script.

Pacific Islands Monthly
    1973   "Peace not PACE in Eniwetok," Vol. 44, no. 7, July.

Richard, Dorothy E.
    1957   *United States Naval Administration of the Trust Territory of
            the Pacific Islands.* vol. III, Washington, D.C.: Government
            Printing Office.

Riesenberg, Saul H.
    1954   *Report on Visit to Kili.* Office of the High Commissioner,
            U.S. Trust Territory of the Pacific Islands: Typescript.

Rynkiewich, Michael A.
    1972   *Land Tenure Among Arno Marshallese.* Ph.D. dissertation,
            University of Minnesota.

Schneider, Harold K.
    1970   *The Wahi Wanyaturu: Economics in an African Society.* Vik-
            ing Fund Publications in Anthropology, no. 48. Chicago: Al-
            dine Press.

Spoehr, Alexander
    1949   *Majuro, A Village in the Marshall Islands.* Fieldiana: Anthro-
            pology, vol. 39. Chicago Museum of Natural History.

Tobin, Jack
    1953   *The Bikini People, Past and Present.* Majuro, Marshall Islands:
            Mimeographed.

    1954   *Kili Journal.* Majuro, Marshall Islands: Mimeographed.

    1957   *Kili Project Survey.* Majuro, Marshall Islands: Typescript.

    1958   "Land Tenure in the Marshall Islands." In *Land Tenure Pat-
            terns: Trust Territory of the Pacific Islands.* Office of the
            High Commissioner, Guam.

United Nations
    1956   *Report on the Trust Territory of the Pacific Islands.* New
            York.

U.S., Department of State
    1968   *Bulletin* vol. LIX, no. 1525. Washington, D.C.: Government
            Printing Office.

U.S., Department of State
    1972   *Trust Territory of the Pacific Islands 25th Annual Report to the United Nations.* Washington, D.C.: Government Printing Office.

Wenkam, Robert and Byron Baker
    1971   *Micronesia: The Breadfruit Revolution.* Honolulu: East-West Center Books, University of Hawaii Press.

Wiens, Herold J.
    1962   *Atoll Environment and Ecology.* New Haven and London: Yale University Press.

U.S. TRUST TERRITORY
CORRESPONDENCE AND DOCUMENTS

1946
1947   United States Navy Department, Military Government Unit, Kwajalein, Marshall Islands. Quarterly Reports. Mimeographed.

1947   Records of Proceedings of a Board of Investigation Convened at the U.S. Naval Military Government Unit, Kwajalein, Marshall Islands by Order of Chief Military Government Officer Marshalls Sub-Area to Investigate the Proposed Resettlement of the Bikini-Rongerik Natives, June 2, 1947.   Mimeographed.

1948
1949   United States Navy Department, Civil Administration Unit, Majuro, Marshall Islands. Quarterly Reports. Mimeographed.

1956   Verbatim Account of Public Meeting; Marshallese People and United Nations Visiting Mission, March 7, 1956. Majuro, Marshall Islands: Mimeographed.

1956   Letter to High Commissioner from J. Tobin, District Anthropologist, October 17, 1956.

1956   Verbatim Account of High Commissioner's Meeting with Bikini people, prepared by Marshalls District Anthropologist, November 10, 1956. Majuro, Marshall Islands: Typescript.

1960   Marshalls District Field Trip Report, December 16, 1960. Majuro, Marshall Islands: Mimeographed.

1961   Memorandum to Distad Marshalls from Assistant Distad Marshalls, April 16, 1961. Majuro, Marshall Islands: Typescript.

1969   Letter to High Commissioner from Kili Magistrate, December 14, 1969.

Index

acculturation *3, 16, 18-19, 90, 95, 99, 100, 143-144, 155, 188, 193, 197*
adoption *42, 51, 55-56, 120, 123, 163, 167*
Ailinglablab Atoll *21, 44-45, 106, 161, 164, 183*
Alkire, William *4*
applied anthropology *8, 85-88, 110-111, 118, 132-133*
Atomic Energy Commission *147, 175, 177, 179*
Barnett, Homer G. *vii, 9*
Bikini Atoll
    environment of *3, 11, 12, 16-18, 21, 23, 27, 83, 175*
    Golden Age *111, 148, 178, 191*
    legal disposition of *116, 139-142, 182, 199-201*
    nuclear test site *3, 26-28, 31, 78-80, 83-84, 87, 147-148, 175*
    rehabilitation of *177-181*
    return to *9, 80, 82-84, 96, 111, 140-141, 147-148, 151, 173, 175-184, 191*

Bikini community
    communal organization *85-86, 107, 112-113, 118-119*
    council *22, 64, 66-68, 81-83, 85-86, 89-90, 99-100, 104, 108, 120, 136, 161, 163,*

    167, 189, 173
demographic structure *39-45, 49, 60-61*
discord/conflict *57-66, 116-117, 121, 123-124, 132, 162-168, 173, 176, 179, 188*
early history *16*
endogamy *46*
expatriots *42-45, 50, 105, 113, 120-121, 126, 155, 157, 161, 164, 166, 178, 182-183, 190*
kinship *5, 46-51, 57, 81, 121*
marriage *18, 42, 42-46, 48-51, 55, 58-60, 155, 157, 165-166*
political structure (*see* Bikini community council and land tenure)
population size *12, 16, 39, 105, 145, 147, 149, 155-156, 178, 183*
relocation, attitudes *3, 28, 34, 81, 97, 111, 114, 128*
self-image *19, 37, 90, 114, 143-144, 152, 155, 193*

Caroline Islands *12, 13*
Central Intelligence Agency *196*
clans
    functions of *37-38, 81*
    sub-clan defined *38*
commercial activities
    community store *22, 78, 81,*

209